# LOVING
*the*
# SPACE
*You're In*

LIZ VINCIGUERRA

ISBN: 978-1-957723-50-1 (hard cover)
      978-1-957723-51-8 (soft cover)

Edited by: Erika Nein

Published by WARREN Publishing
Charlotte, NC
www.warrenpublishing.net
Printed in the United States

*This book is dedicated to anyone who wants to make changes to their living spaces. Beautiful, functional, organized rooms make for a happy, less stressful life!*

# ACKNOWLEDGMENTS

First and foremost, a heartfelt thanks to my all my children—Greg, Clarissa, Ana, and Luke—who support, encourage, and love me always. You have been, and continue to be, a source of great joy, personal growth, and inspiration.

Lucy, I am grateful you took me under your wing and taught me at such an impressionable young age how to make a bed, clean, iron, and utilize sanitary practices in the kitchen.

Thank you to my cousin Carol whom I am truly blessed to spend so much time with working side by side helping others and making a positive impact in their lives.

I would also like to thank the team at Warren Publishing for all their guidance and professionalism throughout this publishing process to make this resource guide available to the marketplace. Erika and Katherine, thank you for your editing and help in making this book sparkle and shine! I appreciate you, your feedback, and expertise.

Last, but never least, thanks be to God, who wants the best for us always and truly wants us all to be happy.

# TABLE OF CONTENTS

# CHAPTER 1

## Taking Back Control of Your Life

Do you ever look around your home and feel defeated? Has clutter climbed its way into every nook and cranny? Has your unique sense of style been buried by disorder? When you are constantly running around, it's difficult to maintain a home that is functional and organized—never mind one that is beautiful and brings you peace. To find your inner designer and create a home that supports and embodies who you are, you must have a practical understanding of how your space is being used and come up with a plan to optimize function and form. It will, for sure, take time and elbow grease to clear out and clean out, but you don't have to spend a lot of money decorating your space to reflect what's important to you. In fact, you can work with what you already own. The tranquility you will gain from having a harmonious home will be well worth the effort!

So how can you get started on the path to loving the space you're in? Look around your spaces. How do they make you feel?

Our surroundings and their cleanliness affect our moods, productivity, and energy levels. Think about how walking into a messy bedroom at night feels compared to entering a clean hotel room on your first day of vacation. Even if you aren't on vacation, that hotel room evokes a great vibe because it is tidy and clutter-free. You don't need to go on vacation to have that calming, welcoming feeling every time you come home or go to sleep!

As an adult, you quickly come to realize how much of your daily existence is completely out of your control, and it can be frustrating to feel like life and the universe are constantly conspiring against you. Reorganizing your environment—creating a sense of order, clarity, and peace to support your current or changing lifestyle—is one of the few things you *can* control.

We all respond to our surroundings. These responses produce chemicals in our bodies that can make us feel relaxed, healthy, and happy ... or stressed, anxious, and depressed. Rooms can be a lot like the people we encounter: they can either uplift us or drain us completely. A lot of factors in a space can evoke an emotional and physical response from us on some level, no matter how small. Below I touch upon some of these factors—many of which are in our direct control—but we will dive into them further in subsequent chapters.

Half the battle in creating a space that supports you is getting it in good order and decorating it in a way that makes you feel happy. The other half is getting in the daily habit of putting things away and undertaking some quick cleaning practices to ease your days ahead. (If you really hate cleaning, see if you can pinch pennies elsewhere and hire someone to do it for you and just do the main wiping and vacuuming in the traffic areas and easy-to-reach places.)

## Color and Lighting

Color impacts mood. It can help create a more intimate, inviting space and can also be used to help reflect more of the natural lighting available; think wall color and paint finish. Changing the color scheme or adding an accent color with a rug, pillows, or throw blanket can really change the vibe of the room. Painting your walls will give you a big change in how your room looks overall because of the large visual real estate that walls take up. Several apps are available where you can upload a picture of your room and explore paint color options, so you can get an idea how a new color will look before you paint. Paint finish is also referred to as paint sheen. Flat paint, or matte, has no shine and is very forgiving in older homes. It is usually used on low-traffic walls and ceilings that won't need cleaning or scrubbing. Doors, trims, and cabinets are often high- or semi-gloss sheens. The shinier the paint, the easier it will be to keep clean. Bathrooms have high humidity concerns, and flats aren't recommended here. Paint store professionals will help you determine the best finish for your space, but I do recommend getting pint-size samples of your color choices, so you can check how they look by painting a test square on your wall before you commit to the whole room. Give yourself twenty-four hours to see how you like the color samples.

Lighting also has a direct impact on mood, so much so that you can buy special lamps and light bulbs to mimic daylight to help with fatigue at your desk or seasonal affective disorder. Natural lighting is always a great source to light a space, but often we need to filter the outdoor lighting that enters our homes, and we need to bring in artificial light to darkened spaces. The lighting we choose has a great impact on the look of the space and how well the space functions. Adding decorative floor lighting and directing it upward onto a wall creates a dramatic, artistic look and is something I like during the darker winter months to keep living room areas brighter in the evening. Try placing one in a corner behind a taller plant and see what you think. It's an easy and inexpensive way to personalize a space and lighten things up. Think of how fun and happy white Christmas lights make the home feel during the darker winter month of December.

Rachel and Stephen Kaplan, former psychology professors at the University of Michigan, conducted a study on lighting and psychology called *The Experience of Nature: A Psychological Perspective*. They found that light has biological and psychological effects that can improve mood and stabilize our circadian rhythms, enabling a better night's sleep, as well as decrease depression scores, and even increase cognitive performance, such as reaction time.[1]

## Smell

Do you remember walking into your childhood home and smelling cookies baking in the oven, or perhaps it was your favorite dinner? The memories of these experiences, just like the real thing, evoke pleasant responses and boost endorphins. Compare those aromas to the foulness of an overflowing garbage can or the stench of a skunk; the response is not the same! Smell has a huge psychological impact, whether we are conscious of it or not. Candles, incense, and flowers can help your home smell and look great, and we will discuss this further, but the foundation of a good-smelling space is a clean space. **TIP: If you smell damp mildew, you need to find the source and correct it. Never mask it with a plug-in air freshener or incense.**

## Noise

Sometimes my home is quiet and peaceful, allowing me to rest. Sometimes the streets outside are loud and busy—especially during certain times of the day—and this can annoy and frustrate me.

---

1 Rachel Kaplan and Steve Kaplan, *The Experience of Nature: A Psychological Perspective* (Cambridge, Cambridge University Press, 1989).

Compare how you feel when you are in the car listening to your favorite playlist with hearing your boisterous neighbors that you simply cannot tune out. Noise, for better or worse, affects our moods. The good news is, you do have some control over the noise levels in your own space.

Noise influences our comfort levels, so think how you might make the noise in your environment more supportive. Perhaps something like changing the bathroom exhaust fan to one that is a quieter decibel level can help you start your day in a more comfortable way. Maybe a fan can be utilized to drown out exterior noise. Incorporating music is one of the easiest ways to minimize unpleasant sounds, and it can be an inviting jump start to your day. (Just be courteous and don't play it too loudly!)

## Air Quality

Most people would agree that temperature and humidity are environmental factors that also directly relate to our comfort and moods. Air quality is equally important. A stuffy, dusty, bacteria-ridden room can wreak havoc on our bodies and slowly, over time, make us feel lousy without even knowing why. Clean, fresh air is important to our health, so be sure to open your windows and let the breeze flow through your home every so often. Use fans to circulate the air, and be sure to change or clean the air filters in your home to maximize the air quality in your living spaces.

The good news is that you absolutely can change your surroundings—and more easily than you think. Keep reading!

## How to Make this Book Work for You

All of your belongings need a proper place of storage. That place needs to make sense, be close to where the item will be used, and make said item easy to grab and use. It also should enable you to quickly and easily return the item to its "home." In the following chapters, I will walk you through how to tackle that.

You don't *have* to start at the beginning of the book, but I recommend you do so. Beginning with the easiest spaces first will help keep you motivated and give you some momentum to keep moving toward a clutter-free life. **TIP: The top three clutter problems people face tend to be laundry (see chapter 6), accumulating piles of paper (see chapters 8 and 9), and keeping the kitchen clean and clear (see chapter 7). You may want to save those chapters for last.**

Commit to one chapter at a time and complete any homework assignments before moving on to the next, for instance, returning items to rightful owners and taking out the trash. One chapter a week is a good, casual goal. Obviously, two per week will get you there twice as quickly. Move through your spaces as swiftly as

*Throughout this process, remember to move quickly and go with your first response. Shoot for good enough; perfection is exhausting!*

you feel motivated! Once an area is completed, keeping it clean and clear of the clutter that seems to creep in on all of us will be easier.

The guidelines provided for you are easy to remember and implement. Some tips and tricks are repeated, so let them become your new mantras as you recreate your spaces. These new mantras, tools, and habits will have a huge positive impact on your quality of life, and you will develop more supportive habits as you read along! I expect that when you have finished this book, you'll take less time to get ready at the start of the day, bills will be paid on time, and you will even be more decisive in your day-to-day decision-making. Most importantly, you will have a space that you love to come home to. (You will also feel much better about unexpected knocks at your door, because you won't be embarrassed by the lack of order or cleanliness in your space!)

By putting in the effort, your hard work will enable you to live the emotionally and physically clutter-free life that you deserve. The initial time investment toward clearing the clutter will free up valuable time and resources later, allowing you to spend the bulk of your time doing things you enjoy with the people you love, rather than looking for misplaced keys or scrambling to pay a past-due bill. Making even minor adjustments as you clean and clear your environment will help you to live a happier, healthier, richer, more productive, and more rewarding life.

You are ready for this! Just start with one chapter. Enjoy the process and your progress, and know you are developing new habits and new organization systems that will serve you well. Congratulations on taking the first step.

# CHAPTER 2

## *Your Ride*

---

### Supplies Needed

- ❏ Glass cleaner
- ❏ Interior car cleaner
- ❏ Paper towels
- ❏ Vacuum
- ❏ 2 buckets: one with warm, soapy water; one with clean water for rinsing
- ❏ Stiff brush (old toothbrush or a stiff, nonstick scrub sponge)
- ❏ 5 cotton ear swabs
- ❏ Squeegee
- ❏ Rags (old washcloths, towels, socks, shirts)
- ❏ 4 sturdy cardboard boxes (small to medium in size)
- ❏ Marker
- ❏ Garbage bags

*I* recommend that you start your clutter-free journey with your car, if you have one. If you don't, feel free to skip to the next chapter.

Cars are relatively small and self-contained, so beginning the process here will keep you energized to keep going each and every day—think leveling up in a game, or upgrading to 3.0 version of a software. Most of us spend a lot of time in this space, and cleaning it will make your travel time more pleasant. You deserve to drive in style and comfort!

Have you ever been inside a new car? If not, you can go to a dealership and sit in one just for the experience. (Try not to let the salespeople get to you while you're there.) Believe it or not, it's possible to recapture that fresh, new-car feeling. You will find that once you have made your car more organized and developed new habits to keep it that way, traveling really gets easier and much more pleasant.

Having a clean and organized vehicle is something you're going to notice and appreciate. Plan on an hour for the interior, less if you're superfast, and an hour for the exterior, in that order. If you need to spread it out over two days to make it more manageable, do so. If your car is a real mess, you can break the cleaning down into three areas: clearing out and sorting all the junk, then cleaning the interior, and lastly, cleaning the exterior. Take a day for each task, if need be, but do NOT spend all day doing this! Your goal is to make it better, not perfect, by doing your best for a short burst. Perfectionism is the biggest roadblock for most of us; let's get rid of that word and mindset, and focus on making things *better*.

### Clearing Out the Interior Clutter

To begin clearing out your vehicle, first grab your marker, four cardboard boxes, and garbage bags. The boxes should be small to medium in size so they are easy to manage and won't take up a ton of room. Remember, the idea is to clear as much out of your life as you can, not just organize and keep everything. Label the boxes as follows:

- KEEP & MOVE. This box will be used to return items from your house to their proper locations. This is for something like a sweatshirt, travel mug, or anything else that normally belongs inside your home but happens to be in your vehicle.
- STAYS PUT. This one is for things that will stay in your vehicle. It will have a permanent home in your trunk, so you might want to use a medium-size box for this.
- DONATE. This box will go back into your trunk so you can drop the items off for donation. For example, I bag clothes to donate, label precisely what the bag is, and place it in the box.
- RETURNS & ERRANDS. This box could include anything someone else left behind during a visit, something that you borrowed or bought that must be returned such as some library books or CDs, or perhaps a jacket that has to go to the dry cleaner. You get the idea. Do not take this box into your home! You are working to clear and clean your spaces. Returns and errands require you to take these items someplace away from your home, so you can keep this box on the floor of your front seat as a visual reminder to get it done.

For your two garbage bags, one will be for trash and the other for recycling. **TIP: Once you are done for the day, be sure to get rid of the trash and throw these bags out. If you don't have a recycle container, throw that bag into your trunk, so you can hit the recycling center the next time you're out and about or gassing up at the pump. Don't take it into your home!**

Once you've collected your materials and labeled your boxes, it's time to start emptying your car. Put any loose change or cash you find straight into your pocket! I recommend removing everything from your car first to see what you really want and need to keep in there. Start with the big stuff. Remove any trash on your floors or seats and start sorting items into the designated boxes. You can save cleaning your glove box and any interior consoles for last. Any receipts lying around can go into your KEEP & MOVE box unless you know they are trash. For example, your oil change receipt will be a keeper to sort through later. In fact, if it's easiest for you, grab *all* of the papers in the vehicle and put them into that box and set them aside for now, just to get them out of the way. However, remember to put your important car-related documents back in your glove box.

 If you're in a neighborhood that isn't as safe as you would like, use the buddy system when you wash your car. If it's possible, borrow a friend's driveway in a safer neighborhood to get these tasks done. It would be a shame if you went to the trouble of cleaning your car for your peace of mind, turned your back for a second, and found all of your belongings had been stolen!

Take out the rubber mats. (I love having good, heavy-duty mats that don't slide all over. They will save your carpet from wear and tear and stains. If your mats are shot, think seriously about replacing them in the near future. They will look and perform a lot better.) Next, open the trunk and get rid of all the trash. Separate anything that needs to go back into your home using your labeled boxes.

## The Deep Clean

As soon as everything is outside of your car and in its designated box or bag, if you have access to an outdoor electrical outlet, pull out your vacuum. A wet/dry vacuum cleaner is very handy if you have the garage space to store it, but a regular household vacuum also works well. I try to avoid handheld vacuums and usually get better results from larger ones. (If you don't have either an outlet or a vacuum, another option is using the vacuum at a car wash facility.) Don't forget to vacuum the trunk!

Wash the floor mats with a bucket of warm, soapy water and a stiff brush, rinse them clean, and let them dry in the sun. Once the floor mats are completely dry, put them back in.

Wash all of the windows with a glass cleaner, inside first and then outside. (If you are going to wash the outside of your car on the same day, focusing on the interior surfaces makes more sense.) It's best to do this in the shade if you can for a streak-free finish. Working in the hot sun evaporates the liquid in the cleaner more quickly and can leave residue from the cleaner itself.

Window cleaning is where those mismatched socks, old washcloths or dishtowels, or old T-shirts come in handy. With the socks, slipping one on a hand makes for quick wiping. Paper towels work well too, but they get dirty fast, and you use a lot of them. Just use what you have and don't overthink it, but by using the old T-shirts or wash rags, you can just throw them out when you're done. For me it's a double bonus—I'm getting rid of excess in my home that is not nice enough to donate.

A squeegee makes quick work of exterior window cleaning; it's not something you need to use, but I often take advantage of these at gas stations when I am refueling. If you have a rain repellent product, apply it to your windshield according to the directions. They can really help with visibility if you get a lot of rain in your area.

When you're done washing the windows, wipe all of the interior surfaces with a damp, soapy washcloth and scrub out any stains on your seats or rugs. If you're not sure how a product is going to react with your upholstery, try a small spot in a hidden area first to see if you like it. If you have leather, you can apply a conditioner. Be sure to follow the directions on the product containers and wipe the dashboard down with a car interior protectant. For those hard-to-reach spaces like the air vents and the corners of the cup holders, I use cotton ear swabs. If you have a can of compressed air that you use for your computer, you can also use that here, but ear swabs dampened with soapy water work just as well.

### Filling the Interior Consoles

Now, examine the pile of stuff you've removed from your car and put back only what you need. Start with the center console between the driver and passenger seats. I keep napkins here and maybe a small hand lotion or a baggie of miscellaneous smaller items. I use freezer baggies and group similar items together. It's easier for me if everything is corralled, and if something should leak or melt in the sun, it won't leak all over the car, just into the baggie. The freezer-grade bags are made with a heavier plastic and are sturdier. I prefer to use them because these bags will take a beating. But any baggie is better than no baggie at all with the added bonus that I can easily see the contents.

If, when you were initially cleaning out your car, you found a lot of loose change, you could keep an unbreakable jar in the vehicle to store the coins in as you accumulate them. The container should have a lid that screws on to prevent spills. If you want to cut a slot in the middle so you don't have to open it up when you put change into it, have at it. And if you find any dollar bills on the floor, you can send those to me!

One other tool I like to keep nearby at all times is a compact fiber dusting wand to periodically wipe my dashboard off when it starts to look dusty. I store it in the pocket behind the passenger seat where it's easy to reach, and with a few swipes all the dust is gone, and the car looks great when you're between cleanings. Your local dollar store may have these.

When organizing your glove compartment, put back only what you need, with a focus on keeping it to a minimum. I recommend using the glove compartment for your car manual and an envelope or baggie that contains your registration and insurance cards. You could keep a tire pressure gauge here as well, but it's not necessary since air pumps at the gas station have them built in. I have a few straws in my glove compartment just in case, and one package containing a napkin, spoon, and fork. The operative word here is *one*, not ten—that just clutters things up!

I keep a box of tissues in the middle of the back seat and also have a plastic bag in my car for trash since I am on the road often. I like to keep some plastic grocery bags in the pocket behind the passenger seat in my car, so if I find myself with unexpected, messy trash, I have someplace to put it quickly that keeps the rest of my car clean. I drape the one I am using over the gear shifter, but it stays light and not too full, and I don't drive a stick shift. I also make sure to get rid of it daily.

### Organizing the Trunk

Next, we're moving on to the trunk. I keep two milk crates in mine. If milk crates are unavailable, that medium-size box you have, or a square basket, will keep your items from sliding all over the place. The container doesn't really matter, it just needs to comfortably fit in the trunk without taking up too much space. You can also search for containers made specifically for organizing your car. I use my cardboard boxes and crates to organize my insulated shopping bags, a first aid kit, at least one paper towel roll, flares, a flashlight, an ice scraper, a small blanket, an accordion file folder with store coupons, a file for my maintenance and receipts for the vehicle, and extra windshield washer fluid. The trunk is also where you will keep the STAYS PUT box.

### The Exterior

Cleaning the outside of your vehicle will be last. If you're running out of time, you can do this another day. The easiest way to clean the outside of your car is to take a trip to the car wash. I'm not big on using the hose in the backyard and waxing my vehicle there— it's hard to reach the top of the car, and for me, the car wash is superfast. I use the drive-through, but that won't work if you drive a convertible! But if you have a hose and like to wash by hand, grab a bucket, soap, and a sponge that won't scratch your car's surface, and have at it. If you do wash by hand and you live where winters are rough, think about going through the car wash occasionally to get the salt and sand cleaned off of the underside of your car.

Once the exterior is washed, use the paper towels or old T-shirts in your trunk to dry off certain areas. I like to open the car doors and wipe down the edges of the doors, as well as any other place where I can see water pooling. Do the bottoms of the doors last, because they are filthy! You will need lots of rags because you don't want to smear the dirt around; you want to wipe it off. Once the doors are dry, go to the trunk and do the same thing to any areas where you can see water and dirt collecting. Finally, if you are up to it, pop the front hood and do the same thing where you can.

*A general theme throughout this book is to make things easier for yourself by doing something each day to make tomorrow better. If that means splurging on a car wash, so be it.*

If you can, hit the hood and the roof with a quick wax treatment. You're not trying to make a marathon of this project, but applying a protective coating now while it's clean will go a long way in keeping your car looking good. The top surface of the car gets a lot of sun exposure and debris, wearing it down; so if you neglect to wax it, the paint will start to peel and wear away. Follow the manufacturer's directions and do this in the shade as directed.

Cleaning your tires is a task you will most likely only do once a year or if they still look dirty after the exterior has been washed. If you don't have time, reserve another day to tackle this task.

If you like the smell of an air freshener in your car, now is the time to treat yourself and get one. I have found that I don't need to open them all the way when they are new, and I personally wait a few weeks to completely remove the wrapper. Opening the air freshener all at once can be a bit overwhelming for my liking.

Lastly, don't forget to throw out those dirty rags. No sense putting them in with your wash and ruining your clothes with the grease they may have collected. And by using them for this purpose, you've already recycled them before they went straight to the trash.

## Maintenance

After the first deep clean, it should be easy to maintain your car consistently by vacuuming it out whenever the floor mats start to look like they have accumulated noticeable debris on them. That does mean you'll need to remember to take a look at them every few weeks. If you can, it's good to hit the automatic car wash every few months. Many of them have vacuums available, making vacuuming out your ride easy and fast. Be sure to wash the outside whenever it starts to look dirty. Consider treating yourself to a professional detail at least once in your car's lifetime. The detail is worth the investment, and it looks great. A good detailer cleans everything inside and out from shampooing the rugs and waxing the exterior, to applying leather or vinyl protectant to the interior. You can always price this out before you clean your car and decide if you just want to clear out the trash and sort the clutter so a detailer can do his job. Hiring a detailer is a quick and easy way to get a professional result. If your headlights are looking very scratched and dull, you can get these done separately by the same folks you would call to fix a chip in your windshield—something to seriously consider if night visibility is an issue.

If you do ever get a small chip in the windshield, get the repair done immediately. Costs vary, but most insurance companies will cover that repair, so there's no out-of-pocket expense for you. It takes about thirty minutes. They will often come to you to do the repair. A small chip can spread to become a huge crack, resulting in an expensive windshield replacement.

Don't forget to look at your tires for even wear and possible replacement. They don't last forever, and your oil change attendant may not check these for you.

### Going the Extra Mile: Car Maintenance Logs

This sounds daunting in theory, but in practice it's nothing fancy, just an organized file of maintenance information that I keep in my trunk so I have a handy record. I like to use a large manila envelope for this to store the receipts for repairs or purchases. On the outside of the envelope, I keep a log for my vehicle care noting the date, repair or purchase, cost, and mileage. With this, I can easily determine how long I've gone since the car has had any given item replaced. If I get a part installed with a warranty, I add that information as well. For example, on March 3, 2018, I got four new tires with a 50,000-mile warranty. At the time they were installed, my car mileage was 112,258, so the tire warranty will be valid until the odometer reads approximately 160,000. That particular entry would read:

3/3/18—4 new tires at 112,258 miles. Tire Store. Warranty 50,000 miles. Good through approximately 160,000 miles.

I highlight the "160,000 miles" part so that I can quickly glance at the log about once a month to see if it's time to check something or get an oil change, for example.

TIP: Consult your manual for your car's maintenance schedule. A trustworthy mechanic will remind you when you are due for an oil change or if something looks like it needs to be repaired, but you also probably found a lot of receipts from repairs you've had over the vehicle's lifetime in the mountain of clutter you cleared out. They're in your KEEP & MOVE box, right? Take that box into your house and sort through them at your kitchen table.

Any car repair receipts? Put those in an envelope and make a quick log on the outside by date. For example:

4/22/18—Oil change. Sam's Auto. 115,000 miles. Next change due 120,000 miles.

When you finish making your log, store it in your glove compartment, trunk, or anywhere else in your car that will keep it away from unsightly spills. Mine is large, so I keep it in the trunk box. After that, trash any unneeded papers and file away the ones you need to keep for purchases or work.

Don't get hung up on this if it's all a bit much. You can just keep these receipts in a sturdy manila envelope and sort through them later when you're trying to find a particular record. If I had to choose the most important thing to keep track of, I would pay attention to the oil change sticker the shops put in your upper left front windshield and keep current with that. Your car needs clean oil to run properly and age gracefully. You can check the car's fluid levels periodically yourself between your car's oil changes. The people changing your oil will generally do that for you and top up your windshield-washer fluid and radiator antifreeze if it needs it. Also, keep an eye on tire warranties as well as their wear and pressure. Low tire pressure can cost you fuel efficiency (money) and uneven tire wear (money). Most cars have a gauge for low tire pressure on the dashboard, but tires can wear unevenly from poor alignment too.

Finally, you've gone through a lot of work to clean and clear out your vehicle. Keep it clean by not letting trash pile up. No excuses. Enjoy your clean, comfortable ride!

### Bonus Tips & Tricks

❏ Get rid of donation boxes as soon as possible, preferably on your next trip out. Store them in the trunk initially, so they don't take up space inside the car, unless you need to see it to remember it's there!

❏ Get in the habit of removing trash and recyclables every time you leave your car.

❏ A quick wipe of the interior as often as once a week will keep the car looking great, as will vacuuming when the mats start to look dirty. Remember to vacuum the front and rear dashboards. Sometimes I just pull up to a car wash and use the vacuum for a dollar without using the car wash.

❏ If you get a lot of snow where you live, you should go through a car wash at least at the end of winter to get the salt off the undercarriage of your vehicle. That stuff is brutal and causes rust over the years.

❏ If you work out of your car, get a sturdy plastic file holder that you can easily tote back and forth. I keep one of these behind the passenger seat on the floor so I can grab items quickly. Mine includes a planner, a file for coupons, a file for things that need to go to the post office and stamped envelopes, a receipt log, and a clipboard for meetings with clients.

# CHAPTER 3

## Spa Bathroom Retreat

---

### Supplies Needed

❑ Small- or medium-size container (box, bin, or basket)
❑ Bathroom/tile cleaner
❑ Toilet cleanser
❑ Toilet brush
❑ Rags
❑ Glass cleaner
❑ Plastic bags

---

*A*fter your car is clean and organized, the next area I recommend you tackle is your bathroom—another small and self-contained area.

With regard to cleaning products for this section, I like some cleaners better than others. Organic tub and tile cleaners are good. They are, however, more expensive. You can make some of them at home for pennies, but be careful. Mixing bleach and ammonia will create lethal fumes. You can always buy some empty spray containers, but make sure you label the outside with your homemade contents just to be safe! I frequent discount stores for empty spray bottles and rubber cleaning gloves, as well as other cleaning supplies. I always keep all cleaners stored away somewhere in my bathroom and in the kitchen. This makes for quick, easy cleaning, but for now, just use up what you have.

After removing all the dirty laundry from the bathroom—including towels, floor mats, and shower curtains—and throwing them in the wash, empty the trash can (*every* bathroom should have one) and reline it with a plastic bag. This will keep the trash can clean for you and make removing the trash fast and easy. I also keep my trash can under my bathroom sink, out of sight. Next, head over to the sink area.

## The Bathroom Sink

First, clear the sink counter by putting everything in a small- or medium-size container—a box, bin, or basket would work. Spray cleanser on the counter and sink—don't forget the faucet and handles—and wipe them down. Return only your hand soap, possibly hand lotion, and perhaps a small hand towel to the sink area, if you have room for it. **TIP: Between liquid soap and bar soap, I use liquid because bar soap can get messy fast. If you go the liquid route, consider treating yourself to a decorative hand pump to dispense the soap rather than the store-bought plastic container the soap comes in.** It can pull the room together and usually looks much better than the store-bought containers. Plastic dispensers in the bathroom that look ceramic are my first choice because they don't shatter or chip any floor tiles if they fall, and they will hurt less if they land on your foot!

If your sink area is really tight, you can add a small shelf nearby, but be sure to keep the sink area mostly clear. The less stuff you have on that counter, or any counter for that matter, the easier it is to clean. It is also *much* more sanitary. Did you know that if someone flushes the toilet without closing the lid, those water droplets spray as far as six or seven feet? It's a really great way to spread germs.

Because of this, I recommend that you find a closed cabinet or drawer to store your toothbrush and toothpaste. I keep all of my oral care related items together—including the floss, mouthwash, and mouthwash cups—in a contained area that I need for daily use. It looks much nicer for guests to come in and not see toiletries on the counter, and it's more sanitary. I certainly don't want to brush my teeth with a toothbrush that's been sprayed with droplets of toilet water! Since I use a shelf in my closet for this purpose, I find that a basket is an easy, functional way to keep everything contained and within reach. I store my toothbrush, toothpaste, mouthwash, and floss atop a washcloth or hand towel (something you can wash and replace easily) on the bottom of my basket. I can easily swap out the washcloth, and it keeps the basket clean and dry. You can use the same basket idea (or other type of container) to store your face wash, hair brush, deodorant, perfume, and any cosmetics. Keep it all organized by storing and categorizing like items together in containers that are easy to grab and pull out as needed.

Drawers under your sink, if you have them, are good for things like ear swabs, first aid kits, makeup, razors, and shaving creams—or that small basket for tooth care and gum health. Group them together based on how you use them and store accordingly. I use small clear containers when I can to keep things grouped together, which work well for seeing what's where. Labelers are wonderful, addictive tools for keeping you organized and your space looking polished, but for now let's get you into a routine first, and you can label later.

## The Toilet Area

Clean the top of the toilet bowl tank next. Maybe place a box of tissues here, or an air freshener of some sort is always a good idea. I have seen recipes online for homemade bathroom sprays that mask odors. Store-bought brands are pricey, so you can experiment with making your own with a small travel-size spray bottle. The recipe consists of three ingredients: one part rubbing alcohol to one part water, and about a quarter teaspoon of essential oil. Shake well and spray it in the toilet before and after you go. Here is a good place to use that labeler or simply place on the spray a decorative handwritten label using permanent marker.

Inside and around the toilet is next. This area of the bathroom gets used by everyone and for sanitary reasons needs to stay clean. A regular twice-a-week cleaning of the toilet bowl is recommended to keep it clean, plus giving it a quick clean with a toilet bowl brush and a little cleaner makes it super easy to keep it looking that way.

No one really wants to look at a toilet bowl brush or plunger. If you can, keep these in a closet in the bathroom. If not, get a container that encloses the toilet brush so you don't see the bristles, and keep a plunger somewhere else for emergencies. **TIP: If you don't have pets, I recommend leaving a small bit of liquid cleaner in your toilet brush holder to keep the brush clean. For mine, I put small pieces of leftover soap from the shower and some water in there. I like that it uses up those small pieces of soap that keep dropping to the shower floor and keeps the brush and holder clean.**

Always keep an extra roll of toilet paper nearby and out of sight in case the current one runs out, but I make it my responsibility that a pretty full roll is on the holder. (It's kind of like my car; I don't like to see the fuel gauge dip much below a quarter tank before I fill up again.) I replace my toilet paper roll when it's starting to get very low, and then put the almost-expended roll close by and out of sight so I can use it up and leave the fuller roll for anyone else.

The rest of the toilet paper storage should go somewhere else in the bathroom whenever possible, and yes, always out of sight.

### The Shower/Tub

Next, attack the shower and/or bathtub—and all of those shampoos and soaps. Be ruthless here. You really only need one washcloth, one bottle of shampoo, one bottle of conditioner, and one bottle of body wash or bar of soap. The rest is just clutter and makes for time-consuming cleaning. If you don't shave daily, you probably don't need your razor and shaving cream stored in there either. Store any bubble bath, bath salts, or similar products somewhere else, perhaps under the sink or in your linen closet. If you use an item frequently, keep it nearby with other like items. When a container runs out to the last bit, add a half cup of water, shake, and dilute it so you can get every last drop of product out. When you're done, toss the container in the recycle bin and put a fresh one in to replace it.

Thoroughly clean the surface of the shower or tub unit with your bathroom cleaner of choice. Make sure you rinse all cleaners from any chrome fixtures and drains, wipe them dry, and follow all directions on the packaging carefully. If you don't rinse it well, it will permanently discolor the fixtures, so be very careful. Wash your cleaning rags after you use them.

Sometimes the shower curtain liners can be a pain to keep clean. Some, unless they are completely plastic, can be washed and dried with your towels, but if the seam gets yucky, consider just purchasing a new one. I also have a squeegee mounted on my shower wall for the tile walls (also works well for glass doors/walls), and I wipe the faucets down after use with a dry cloth that I keep in the shower for this purpose. Sometimes I even wipe off the shampoo and conditioner bottles. This may sound like a lot, but it's easy to do and only takes an extra minute because I only keep three product bottles and a bar of soap in the shower. Wiping everything dry cuts way down on soap scum and hard water deposits. It makes future cleanings much easier, plus, as an added bonus, it will always look sparkly clean.

### Additional Surfaces

A clean mirror is a happy mirror. I will spot-clean the mirror several times during the week. Sometimes, just wiping it down with a damp washcloth is all it needs. You can use glass cleaner to give it a deeper clean as often as once a week, but be careful when using your cleaning products. If an ammonia-based cleaner drips down behind the glass, it will ruin the coating. The chemicals from an ammonia-based cleaner can seep around to the back of the glass and react with the back of the mirror, causing black discoloration on the edges of the mirror. There's no way to fix it except to add a trim piece around the mirror to hide the unsightly discoloration. I can't vouch for all commercial products, so use caution when you clean your mirrors, or stick with regular soap and water.

If you have them, your bathroom windows should be kept clean as well. They're easy to do while you are cleaning the mirrors; they naturally don't have to be washed as much. If you keep the windowsill clear, this will be a very quick and easy job.

### Storage and Space

The key to a clean-looking space is to have as many things stowed away in a closet or container as possible and therefore out of sight. Some dwellings have more storage space built in than others. If your home has ample shelving or closet space, all the better. If not, you can install shelving units as needed.

If you have room to add standing shelves or a wardrobe unit in the bathroom, go ahead and get one. Just remember: scale matters! Make sure what you're installing actually fits inside your bathroom without crowding it. Additionally, put small items in a basket or bin to corral them. It looks so much neater and means keeping the shelving unit dust-free will be a breeze.

I prefer to store extra towels on a shelf, folded with the rounded edge facing out. The folded towels look the most visually satisfying to me. Rolled towels in a basket are nice too. Choose what works best for you. Just try to have no more than two towel sets for every person who regularly uses the bathroom, and group all like items together. I like letting each person choose their own color or keeping everything the same color and writing initials along the bottom to designate whose towels are whose. Keep it creative and fun. There is no wrong way to do this. **TIP: I added a removable hook for my towel on the wall next to my shower because the towel rack isn't close. I don't dry my towel here; before my shower I hang the dry towel here so I can grab it quickly and easily when I am ready to dry off.**

### Decorating the Space

Pick a color palette and a theme for your bathroom and stick with it. Bathroom themes often tend to revolve around the beach or water, but anything goes. Pick one set of towel colors and maybe swap them out for a holiday or for a seasonal change. If you have a shower setup that allows for a shower curtain, those can be changed out easily to give your bathroom a fresh new look any time of the year. I switched to a curved shower rod and enjoy the extra elbow room it creates in this space—a definite upgrade in my opinion. If the curtain seems short for where the rod is mounted, consider adding a few inches of matching colored fabric to the hem. Choosing a matching color will be more forgiving of sewing errors. I also added a rain showerhead that looks great and helps me to feel like I've really leveled up in my luxury bathing experience! These come in a variety of price points and may be worth the expense; plus, they are not difficult to install by yourself.

A bath mat can be neutral or match your towels as closely as possible. Remember, a bathroom rug or mat isn't necessary. If you're short on funds, you can always use an extra towel on the floor for this. If you do buy one, be sure to measure it and make sure it fits your bathroom. Size *does* matter! You want the mat to fit in place and match the color scheme of the room without overtaking it entirely.

Adding a custom liquid soap dispenser really does give the bathroom a visual upgrade, and it's easy to keep full. You can even use body wash to fill them up or any shampoo you don't like, just don't use the purple shampoo that's made for gray and blonde hair unless you want a mess and stained towels!

If you have a window in the bathroom, make sure you have privacy! My personal preference in the bathroom is a valance, which allows for more lighting. You can use a shade for privacy and forgo the curtain entirely, which is also a nice option. If your window dressings are old, ripped, or stained, replace them. Another option is vinyl sheets that adhere to your window glass. These provide privacy while still letting the light in, and a white one with a valance shows well. I've had an issue with getting some brands of window films to stay in place and not curl. (I ended up using a lighter-grade white plastic that looked great and worked well.)

I see lots of magazines and book racks and collections in people's bathrooms. I am personally not a fan. They just give you more items to clean around, and they clutter up those clean, clear surfaces. I say do your business and get out. If you want to read, find a more relaxing and peaceful place to do it! Enough said here.

I like to keep a small clock in the bathroom to keep me on schedule. A clock radio can be nice for music and news if you like that. I also have a night-light in my bathroom. They're great for overnight guests, if you have young children at home, or if you tend to use the bathroom in the middle of the night. It's a lot nicer to have a soft night-light than having to turn on a bright room light.

If you have a fan to vent the bathroom and it is noisy, consider changing it to a low-decibel fan. A noisy fan can be annoying, but if it's on the same switch as the light, there is no avoiding it. (The fan is there for an important purpose. If you don't have a window you can open to get rid of the humidity, definitely use the fan.) They are not particularly expensive—the lowest price fans are the noisiest—but if the noise will bother you, look at the decibel level and pay the extra money; it will be well spent! You may need someone to install the new fan for you.

A plant—either real or fake, depending on your level of gardening prowess—adds lots of personality to a space. They are surprisingly easy to care for in the bathroom, since the close proximity to the faucet makes watering them easy. Keep in mind the amount of sunlight your bathroom normally gets when you choose the type of plant to buy. If the plant starts to look very unhappy, please move it to another location.

If you have a small sink area in your bathroom, only put a small plant, candle, or decorative item there so you can still accommodate your hand soap. It also looks great when you limit that counter space to just the hand soap and a hand towel. A plant or candle can look just as pretty on the windowsill or a shelf, just be careful of curtains and any open flame. I am not a big fan of candles on the top of toilet tanks, but I see it all the time. It's one of my pet peeves. I somehow envision that one day someone's hair is going to catch fire!

Freshly cut flowers can be nice too. If you can find a nice-looking plastic vase, all the better, just in case it ever gets knocked over, but I save fresh flowers for other rooms in my house. There are artificial plants and flowers that look amazing and can help create the spa feeling we all love, just remember: more is not always better. I personally have a silk lavender plant that I drop essential oil on that sits on top of my toilet tank. It works perfectly for my space, so don't let a lack of lighting deter you from adding some greenery here. It makes the bathroom look especially lovely. Succulents can even work well tucked on a small shelf. Again, the plants don't have to be real, and you don't want big plants unless the bathroom is a large one and there's room for a floor tree, but real ones do give the place a nice, fresh touch. Keep in mind, some artificial plants look a lot more real than others and have zero watering maintenance.

I have found that a small piece of art can also go a long way in a bathroom. Choose something that makes you smile when you look at it on the wall and matches the overall color scheme of the room. This is one of the first rooms you'll spend time in when you start your day and one of the last rooms you spend time in when you end it, so pick something you love. Remember to keep the color and theme in mind, and choose something the right size for the room. It's probably easiest to base your color theme around the shower curtain you have chosen. Monochrome color schemes work great in small bathrooms because they tend to make a space look larger. (For more ideas, see the Small Spaces sidebar in chapter 5.) You could even add an accent wall of large-graphic floral in powder rooms, but that's not for everyone—certainly not if you're renting!

Keep cleanliness and simplicity as your main theme, and always consider the scale of the bathroom in question when deciding what to add and what to omit. By now, your bathroom should look and smell amazing, like a spa retreat. Enjoy starting and ending your day in a beautiful, clean, sparkling space. You deserve it!

### Bonus Tips & Tricks

❑ If you splatter on the mirror, use the hand towel and wipe it up immediately with a little water.

❑ Quickly cleaning the toilet, sink, and shower every week can go a long way. If this is too much at once, moving forward, always keep the sink clear, and then it is just a matter of scrubbing the toilet one day and cleaning the shower another. This may be all the cleaning you need to keep your bathroom ready for use or company!

# CHAPTER 4

## Entryways

---

### Supplies Needed

- ❑ Broom
- ❑ Vacuum
- ❑ A decorative eye

---

*L*et's tackle the entry area on its own. This includes the front door and back door, both inside and out. It could also include a small hallway. This is the first place your guests see when they come over, and it's an important area most people ignore. Some properties have more than one point of entry, so you can take a couple of days to divide up the labor between them if you're pressed for time. The goal for this chapter is to make each entry to your home as welcoming and functional as possible. This is a fast and easy area to master that doesn't require very much upkeep, so let's get started.

## The Front Porch

If your house has a front porch, having a small table and seating can really make this spot look inviting and welcoming. If you choose to use pillows on the chairs, be sure to get something waterproof. Some people like to hang a flag in this area by the front door; however, it's important to keep it simple. Military flags are nice but do have their own rather strict guidelines. If they start to look worn or faded, replace or remove them. If you want to keep plants on your porch, invest in an inexpensive side table or shelf so you don't have a lot of small pots just sitting on the ground, or aim for fewer, larger pots instead. A macrame plant hanger is not a difficult DIY. If you do make it yourself, use black twine. It always looks great and never looks dirty! Window boxes, if your setup allows it, can also look very nice. Just remember, if you have plants, they will need watering and occasional pruning, and eventually may need some fertilizer. If you'd like to add a wreath or hanging decoration to your door, make it proportionate to the size of the door itself, and make sure it's centered well and isn't obstructing any window elements your door may have. For safety reasons, you need to be able to see out your front door.

Porches, and even front steps on their own, need to be swept every so often. It's up to you to determine how often is often enough, but if it's close to a tree or bush that sheds frequently, it may be a good idea to permanently store a broom on the porch in a discreet location. If you prefer a folksy, country-style look to your porch area, some brooms can be put on display as a functional artistic piece, but I prefer to keep them hidden from view.

If your porch or doorway has stairs or even a ramp leading up to it, it is imperative to keep this path clear of any items! It cuts back on visual clutter and is much safer. There is especially no reason to store items on a ramp, since you aren't even dealing with a level surface. If you're using a designated pathway to store anything at all, you're going to want to find a better spot for whatever's there.

The only thing that is acceptable to have in front of your doorway is a welcome mat for wiping off your feet on the way in. I strongly encourage you to invest in a good one and not the tiniest one they sell; the reasons will become apparent soon.

Some people have balconies, which I like to treat as a porch of sorts. It might not be used as frequently, but it should be swept regularly and kept relatively free of clutter. Both are seen from the street, so it's always important to keep those areas tidy and inviting!

**The Entry and Exit**

I often go to my door with my hands full. Whether it's grocery bags, a purse, a laptop, keys, or something else entirely, there's always something in my hands when I'm leaving or entering my house. It's likely that there's usually something in yours too. Since it's a lot easier to open the door when my hands are free, I used to end up putting these things on the ground. One day, I decided enough was enough, and I finally put a small table next to both the interior and exterior side of my door. Ever since then, I've found I can more quickly and easily get in and out of the house because I'm not bending down to pick things up off of the ground, and I can set them there if needed when unlocking or locking the door. I did add one small knickknack to the top of this table, just because it looked nicer than leaving it empty. It's something fun that makes me smile. **TIP: Surround yourself with things that you love and are functional for your life and your space. Not everything in your living space necessarily needs to be useful!**

Remember how I suggested putting a welcome mat on your porch? You're going to definitely want to have one at least on the outside, and preferably one on the inside as well, because it makes a huge difference in keeping dirt and debris out of your home. Make sure to measure the area in front of your door so you get the right size, just the way you did with your bath mat. The idea with the outdoor mat is to keep as much dirt outside of the home as you can, so you'll have to do less cleaning inside later! The smallest mat is not a good idea, because lots of folks will not really be wiping their feet on it, but rather just walking across it. For this reason, you want to get a larger mat.

Not all of the dirt will be left on your outside front door mat, so it is a good idea to put a decent sized area rug on the inside of your door as well. A second mat means you can get even more dirt or moisture off of your shoes as you enter, and less dirt will get further into your space. It's especially important during winter months, because if you get a lot of snow, you're going to want to keep as much of it off your floor as possible.

It will keep your space cleaner if you can get in the habit of taking off your shoes when you get home. No need to track in dirt from the outside all over the inside. Trust me when I say, the grooves on the soles of your shoes will release dirt long after you walk in if they stay on your feet. Do yourself a favor and take them off as soon as you can, and if it's an option, create a spot for your shoes by the door. Obviously, not everyone is going to take their shoes off all the time, and I certainly don't expect houseguests to take their shoes off, but you will notice a difference in your home of how much cleaner things look and stay if everyone gets into the habit of removing their shoes.

I end up sweeping or vacuuming the front entryway at least once a week or when I can visually see it being necessary. I vacuum my indoor mat more frequently than the outside mat. Patterns in the carpeting are much more forgiving, and I take advantage of this decorating tip by keeping a patterned rug on the inside of my entry doors, so I don't constantly see the dirt on it between vacuuming. The outside mat is a gray/black solid color with ridges and has a waterproof backing. I don't recommend solid light colors at all. You can tell those are dirty right away!

Lighting is critical at any point of entry in your home. Make sure your porch area is well lit, so you can see the doorknob and don't trip over any steps on your way in or out. If you don't have good lighting here, you can buy a battery-operated sensor light so you can quickly and easily get into your home after dark. Check the reviews for a good brand and also check every so often to see if your doorbell is working and that you have a way to see who is at your door before you open it.

I always keep a mirror in this area as well. It gives me an opportunity to take a quick glance at myself before I head outdoors, and I like the added bonus of having it reflect the natural sunlight into my space from the outdoors. **TIP: If you keep anything valuable there, like a tablet or your purse, make sure to lock the door immediately after you enter, so it isn't easy for a thief to grab anything valuable and run out quickly with it!**

---

 If you have pets, keep their water and food bowls, litter boxes, toys, and what have you near the back door as well. You want to keep these items out of the way and out of the line of sight of your guests, and yet have them close enough to maintain them daily. Tucking them away near a back door entry—which usually is in the kitchen, where you have access to water as well as a cabinet for their food and a trash can—makes sense.

Run your vacuum daily. If you don't have one, invest in one—especially if you only have hardwood floors. Vacuums will get the dust out, and they all have floor mode settings. Keep your vacuum out of sight but near an outlet so you can easily plug it in and use it often! Pets drop a lot of hair and dander everywhere, so you will have to stay on top of it if you want your place to look great.

I put a few drops of essential oil on a cotton ball and then use my wand attachment to vacuum up the scented cotton ball into my clean upright each time after I empty the vacuum. This way when I use the vacuum, I can smell the essential oil scent, plus it provides a little extra nice-smell reward for doing some work!

Make sure you are changing any litter box at least twice a week, so your house doesn't stink. Dump the dirty litter in an outside receptacle, and wash the litter box once a month. I'm sure you've heard of the phrase "nose blind," please make sure that's not you!

Additionally, Kitty does go on your kitchen counters no matter what you say, so keep them clear and wipe them down to disinfect before you make that sandwich!

Fish tanks get very dirty and unsightly, so please skip the fish if you can't or won't take the time to keep the water and glass clear and clean.

Birds create a lot of dust and dander and throw seeds everywhere. They can also be very noisy, so if you are in an apartment or condo, be considerate of your neighbors. (I personally enjoy a bird bath and bird feeder in the yard, but not too close to the house so all the spilled bird seed isn't seen!)

Having hooks for coats or hats is extremely helpful. I would keep at least three or four hooks mounted on a wall. I don't like seeing all the coats by the front door, so I keep my hooks mounted by the back door. If you have a back door—since it's not the main point of entry where you'll be receiving houseguests—it's also a good spot to keep trash and recycle bins. Mine are very well-hidden and are covered in a self-contained, freestanding furniture piece. **TIP: Be sure to rinse or wipe out your trash and recycle containers once a week or so, or they will start to smell, and nobody wants to walk into someone's house and smell garbage. I line mine with plastic so I can grab the whole bag on my way to the exterior trash/recycle cans, but it still requires wiping the inside out at least once a month.**

### Decorating the Space

A flowering plant outside can be very welcoming. It adds a lot of color and personality to a space, and like the flowers in the bathroom, it doesn't need to be real if you're not good with gardening. It will definitely need to be rotated out more often than an artificial flower left indoors. Sun damage alone can be brutal. If you choose to add a real plant or mix the two, make sure it's one that flourishes in your area and requires minimal upkeep—unless you are passionate about gardening—and it's something that's easy for you to water. **TIP: It might be helpful to install a cabinet or wardrobe outside of your back entryway for keeping fertilizer, extra pots, and other gardening supplies.**

You also may want to keep a spare key well hidden outside, but that's totally up to you. Just make sure when you fish the spare key out, no one sees the hiding spot. All sorts of knickknacks and compartments are on the market to help hide spare keys, but you can get even more creative. The sky's the limit!

I do like the addition of motion-sensor lighting. You can get a battery-operated light, so when you get to the door at night, you can see what you're doing more easily. Consider these types of lights if you don't have adequate night lighting at your entry; safety is important! Also consider solar lighting for a pathway if the walkway to the door is not well lit. They will last for many years, plus you don't need a lot of them, they don't require an electrician, you can replace the solar batteries when the lights are dim and not as bright (not holding the solar charge from the day), and you can take them with you when move.

---

### Bonus Tips & Tricks

❏ A quick vacuum once or twice a week of the mats will go a long way to keep dirt from entering the house. I store my vacuum near the main entry for this reason and skip the broom; brooms tend to push dirt around. A broom sweep of the porch and steps is better than nothing if it needs to be cleared. Whatever is easiest for you works; just do it if you can see it needs it.

❏ Have a designated spot to keep your shoes after you take them off when you come in.

---

# CHAPTER 5

## The Living Room(s)

---

### Supplies Needed

- ❑ 3–5 boxes for sorting
- ❑ Masking tape
- ❑ Marker
- ❑ Small bucket with warm, soapy water
- ❑ Glass cleaner
- ❑ Washcloth
- ❑ Small towel for polishing
- ❑ Vacuum
- ❑ Trash bags
- ❑ Rags

*N*o matter where you're living, your space is probably going to include a main common room for family gatherings and recreation. For all intents and purposes, we're going to call this area the "living room," although in some smaller homes, this might be combined with a dining room or even a dining room and bedroom. The strategies in this chapter can also be applied to dedicated home theaters, dens, offices, or any other area where you're likely to have a lot of foot traffic.

Let's get to it!

## A Deep Clean

Quickly clear all tables of everything but lighting, and sort knickknacks into the boxes, labeling as you go. Label one box for items that need to be returned to friends or other places, like the library. If there's any trash, put it in the garbage bag immediately. Take any dirty dishes into the kitchen and put them in the sink.

For non-trash items, try to keep similar items together and label the boxes with masking tape that you can remove later if you want to reuse the boxes. If you have a collection, you might want to have a specific box to put the collection in. Think about keeping the collection in the box and storing it—at least for now—and going for a new look to your room. You can always bring it out seasonally, or just pick your three favorites and display them. Grab anything on the floor as well and put it into a box. Get as many surfaces clear as you can. Work clockwise around your room if you're left-handed, or counter-clockwise if you're right-handed. If you're ambidextrous, use the hand you write with the most often to determine which way to start, and commit!

First, if you have curtains, vacuum them to get the dust off. This shouldn't take very long. Wall vents are easy to clean with the vacuum brush attachment (works well on the bathroom vent fan as well). Don't forget to clean ceiling fan blades! A damp cloth works great for this, and keeps the dust from getting everywhere.

Next, clean the windows using your glass cleaner. You want to do this when the sun isn't directly shining through the glass to make the job easier and minimize streaking. Wipe the windowsills while you're there. Next, vacuum the floors and furniture cushions. Once everything has been vacuumed and wiped down, you can start returning items to their spots. If you have window blinds, they are a lot more work to clean. Vacuum them first, and then you can wipe the individual slats with warm soapy water. Some people like to take the blinds down and wash them in the tub or outside, but that seems like more work to me. I leave them on the window.

Now it's time to take the soapy water and wet washcloth and go back around the room cleaning and polishing as you go. You want that cloth damp, not wet, so wring that sucker out! If you can see water droplets when you wipe a hard, flat surface, it's too wet. You'll want to dry the surfaces off as you go, or you'll have smears. You could ruin the surface of your furniture if you leave it wet for too long.

Work your way from the top down. That means you should go around the room, in a clockwise or counter-clockwise fashion, wiping down the tallest pieces of furniture first and gradually going lower as you go. After the tallest shelves and lamps have been wiped down, hit the mid span of the room. If you have pictures on the walls, wipe down the frames to grab any dust. Finally, once those items are all clean, grab that bucket and go for the baseboards. It's likely that you will only have to do a deep clean like this once a year, so go for it. **TIP: You can opt to vacuum the baseboards before you clean them if they are really dusty.**

Now the trash can go right out, and the box of borrowed items can go by the door or in the trunk of your car so you can return them. You want these boxes out so your space is clean, clear, and beautiful! If it all seems too much to tackle, break it into two parts. Get the fan blades, some shelving, and vacuum one day, then save the curtains, windows, and any grimy door trims and baseboards for another day. Shoot for good enough. Perfection is exhausting and sometimes this will mean just vacuuming the main traffic patterns in your spaces. You don't have to clean your baseboards every month, but I do love my vacuum wand to get the corners of my floors or the tops of the door moldings, etc.

## Long-Term Storage

Storing your stuff where you use it saves time and money. It lets you know how much you have of something, and it allows you to easily reach and find it. Once you have your items grouped together, you can evaluate how much storage you actually need for these items. Take what you use, love, and really enjoy, and

*The vacuum is my best friend, so much so that I invested in one of those robot vacuums as well as my regular vacuum. I move it to a different room once a week and am always so surprised at how much it picks up. I still use the upright, but the robot vacuum was a tremendous addition to the family.*

perhaps donate the rest. The less you keep, the less space is taken up, and the less you have to clean and manage. This may not seem like a big deal, but it doesn't do us much good to constantly shuffle things around to get to those items that we really use and love most!

If you have a bookcase, you don't necessarily need to cram every inch of it full of books. You can fill the shelves halfway and save some room in there for a sculpture or a picture frame with a photo in it that makes you smile. You can even turn some books horizontally and stack them vertically in sections of your bookcase. You get the idea—mix it up a bit for visual interest. Bookcases are most aesthetically pleasing when they are not full, so be sure to ask yourself, how many books do you really need to keep? Empty each shelf and/or drawer completely and decide what can stay and what can go, and evaluate if you need to invest in a larger storage system or downsize.

A lot of people keep routers, streaming devices, and game consoles by their television on display, but those things should be tucked away in a cabinet under the TV. The more consoles you have, the more important good cable management is. If you have a lot of different game consoles, it's imperative to have adequate shelving for them all and to keep loose cables tied together so it doesn't look like a mess. My favorite setup involves a cabinet with opaque doors. On the inside of the door, affix a brief tutorial on how to access any console from the television and which remote to use. I also like to hang headphones inside the door with a removable hook. If you don't have a lot of games or media, you can store the cases in the same area as the consoles. However, if you have a very large collection of games, it's best to have a dedicated shelf for them. Any unusual peripherals that take up a lot of space and aren't used as often, like fight sticks or exercise equipment or extra controllers, would be better suited for a chest or drawer. Take it one console at a time, so you're not overwhelmed, and see if there's anything you might want to sell or donate to clear up space.

A table with a clear surface looks immaculate. Keeping your remotes and chargers in a small basket or tray, for example, makes a coffee table look clean and it is, in fact, easier to keep clean. Some coffee tables and couches come with compartments specifically designed for remotes, whereas some people attach fasteners to the underside of a remote and the underside of a table so the remote is out of sight most of the time. This might not work well if you're particularly forgetful or have a glass coffee table. **TIP: If you have more than one remote, label them for guests—as well as for yourself! Having one remote out instead of two cuts down on confusion, so if you're not using the DVD player often, store that remote with the player.**

If you choose to use baskets for the odds and ends, and all of these baskets are the same style, the room will look more put together. An extra throw blanket in the winter can be kept out, but a ton of pillows and throws will look messy fast, and it takes time to keep them looking tidy. My recommendation for that would be an oversized woven basket that you could roll up the extra blankets and pillows and pull them out when needed for movie night or for reading your favorite book. The goal is to clear your space and keep the things you love and love to use where they are used. **TIP: If you don't love it, if it doesn't make you smile, or if it's really worn and tattered looking, get rid of it. Why look at something that isn't uplifting?**

Keep the stairs clear! It's tempting to put items on the steps for people to grab on their way upstairs. But I recommend that you do not place anything on the stairs. Instead, hang a basket on the outside of the railing to keep the floor and steps clear, so they are safe and less cluttered. Pick a basket that is large enough to hold a good quantity of items but small enough to not be difficult to carry. Once it gets full, take it up; take it up each time you go upstairs and empty it; or just grab an item or two on your way up to keep it from overflowing. Keep your floor surfaces clear, unless it's a rug, and table surfaces clear except for a few carefully selected items. No piles allowed!

Once the living room is clean, I mainly just spot clean in specific areas throughout the week when they start to look dusty or something gets spilled. If you have pets or children, you will need to clean more often.

### Decorating the Space

When you choose furniture for these living areas, do your best to stick to one unified theme rather than slapping together a mishmash of styles that don't necessarily work with each other ... unless, of course, that *is* your style, but try and make the look intentional. Think of the focal point in the room. Do you have a fireplace? If so, position the furniture to take advantage of this feature. Perhaps you have a great view of the outdoors. Position the furniture so you can see that! Consider putting a glass-top dining table (round takes up less space) with two chairs by the window, and open your laptop there for work, letting the space serve double duty. This works especially well in small rooms because the glass takes up less visual space. Glass tabletops are less forgiving and will require regular wiping, but they're worth it in a small apartment.

Area rugs can make a space look finished and put together, provide visual interest, and warmth and texture to a space. Rugs need to be large enough to accommodate at least the front legs of your sofa and the coffee table comfortably. If you have additional seating, it's best to place the chair(s) on the rug as well to create a zone and a comfortable area to relax in.

If and when you eventually replace any furniture or lighting pieces, replace them with something that reflects your taste and that is functional for space. Keep in mind the scale of the room as well as the other furniture and colors that are present. Don't get a piece that is so big, it overpowers the space. Does "elephant in the room" ring a bell? Because that is exactly what it can feel like.

*Small* SPACES   If you live in a studio apartment or do not have a lot of square footage, or if you have a very large room, it is a good idea to create zones in that space designating its use: sleeping, sitting, eating, work.

There are plenty of ways to maximize your small space. For example, furniture with legs makes small spaces appear larger by visually tricking your eye. A properly sized sectional takes up less room and creates more space than many smaller chairs. Glass tabletops can help a small space feel more open, but as discussed, it's much harder to keep them looking clean. Round tables take up less room and provide more intimate seating for dining or board games.

Mirrors properly spaced can help create more light and visually open and expand a room's space, but take a look at what view you are reflecting in that mirror. I am not a fan of mirrors over fireplaces because, for the most part, they all provide a view of the ceiling. Unless yours is the Sistine Chapel, I don't recommend this decorating style.

A vertical storage unit will be your best friend in a small space. Knickknacks will not be your friend, so avoid them! It is extremely important to keep your premium counter space clear and uncluttered.

Color theme is always important, especially in tight spots. Choosing a monochrome color scheme will keep your eye from jumping to contrasting colors or bright accent colors. Blues can be tricky and a little hard to match—something to keep in mind. You can use a rug or blanket or piece of art that you love as color inspiration in a room, and by keeping furniture pieces neutral and in solid colors, any room should look more pulled together. You can add texture with pillows or throw blankets and mixed mediums.

If you are using more than one color in a room, remember the 60, 30, 10 rule. The wall color is usually your 60 percent and then another color should make up 30 percent, with perhaps a pop of color in the 10 percent. The tuxedo cabinets are all the rage in the kitchen these days, but keep the darker color on the lower level, or the room will feel unbalanced.

Also, if you can visually see other rooms from the room you are standing in, ask yourself how well the wall colors play together. Smooth color transitions from one room to another are more aesthetically pleasing than strong, contrasting colors. You can get away with breaking this rule in the bathroom or bedroom, but only because those doors are usually kept closed from the rest of the home. If you are going to leave them open, keep this in mind.

If you live in a small space, keep artwork and wall hangings to perhaps one larger statement piece, so the visual backdrop will be more restful and less disjointed. Try not to fill your walls with decorative "touches." Ideally, your eyes need to rest and be drawn to one focal point. Think of artwork or photographs on the walls as rests between notes in music! You want one piece as a focal point, not a ton of pieces scattered randomly about the wall space. Placing art over a couch works, or over dining room seating, but in a really small apartment, that's usually enough. The same goes for artwork consisting of or that has quotes on it. For these to have the greatest impact, keep it to one piece in any room and not more than two in the whole home. Too many words on walls are distracting and don't promote relaxation.

---

Lighting is very important in any space, and the living room is no exception. How you choose to light your room depends in part on how many windows you have and their locations. Sometimes you don't have a lot of options, so you have to figure out a way to work with what you have to get the lighting you need. It's a good idea to first consider how you're going to use the room. Do you like to read in here? Do you need a spot to do homework? Are you constantly watching movies or gaming in this space?

Think about the function and then create the task of setting up lighting that will work for you. For example, you might want a table or desk lamp for homework or bill paying. A tall floor lamp might work great for reading on the couch. Perhaps a soft color or accent light in a corner behind a tall plant for indirect or soft lighting would look nice. A dimmer switch is often a good idea if you own your property or if your landlord allows you to install one. They give you more control over the mood you want to set. On the other hand, you may need to invest in blackout curtains if you're looking at a lot of screens in a room that has harsh lighting. Even when the amount of light the room gets seems like it's out of your control, there are a lot of little things you can do to improve it. Keep in mind the bulb color when you replace them; a bluer light brightens more than a yellowish light bulb.

If you haven't noticed, I love plants! If you don't have plants, I strongly recommend that you get some for your living room. They release oxygen and increase the air quality, and they are good for our psyches and mental health as well, so long as we take care of them and they look good! If you have plants that seem unhappy, check to make sure you are watering them properly. If they are getting enough water, try moving them to another location to make sure they are getting the amount of light they need. They might be too close to an air conditioner or heater vent or may need to be repotted and fertilized. Some plants are easier to take care of than others. Just be sure to get plants that are the right size for your space, that you like the look of, and can be taken care of easily.

As lovely as they look, the more plants you have, the more time and effort it will take to keep them looking great. Real plants need their leaves cleaned once in a while to look their best. The kitchen sink is probably the best place to do this, or if it's a large plant and you can take it outside, all the better. If you have a plant that drops flowers or leaves on the ground often, you'll have to clean around them more frequently than a plant that isn't as prone to shedding. Be sure to look up which plants are toxic if you have pets before buying anything. It's equally important to make sure your plants are not ruining your tabletops, floors, or windowsills. Make sure when you water them the water is not spilling or leaking out underneath.

You *can* have too many plants! If you can't keep them watered and looking great, give some of them away and perhaps try keeping just one or two, and make sure it's a variety that's easy to maintain.

Window treatments can be very expensive but can really change the look and feel of a room. Curtains look best and I prefer them to hang just above the floor by an inch or two, unless you have baseboard heating—you definitely don't want curtains to become a fire hazard! If you love the window treatments you have but they are short, try adding some fabric at the bottom of your curtains and make them longer. You can choose the same fabric color, or see if you like the look of black fabric. Doing this will give your window treatment a more custom look. So often the store-bought standard lengths aren't quite long enough. Extending the length of your curtains can look very elegant. You can try pinning a piece of fabric to the curtain bottoms before you take the time to sew them on and see how you like it. This is your space, but window treatments do have an impact on how the room looks and functions.

Ideally, you want your curtains to be mounted not too far from the ceiling and wider than the window frame. That way, when the curtains are open, you can allow maximum light in while making sure you still can cover the window when you pull them closed. Plus, it makes the windows look larger than they are and the room taller than it is.

A nice summer swap is to hang airy, white panels, and I am a huge fan of the grommet-style curtains. They are super easy to open and close and look great. You can also change out the finials on the ends of your curtain rods to something fancy, or glass for a shiny sparkle!

Windows don't have to have curtains on them, and there are many options for privacy if you want or need that, which most windows will call for. Other options include shades, horizontal blinds, vertical blinds, or the removable vinyl window sheets with or without curtains included.

## Bonus Tips & Tricks

❏ Dust falls, so if you start with taller areas and work your way down, you won't dirty anything you've already cleaned.

❏ Every item in your living room needs to be put in a spot that makes sense. Store it with similar items and put it away when you're done using it.

❏ Keep the floor as clear as possible so you don't hurt yourself tripping over anything, especially near stairs!

❏ Make sure you remember to wipe down the windows. They're easy to forget!

❏ Fan blades have a winter and summer setting to reverse air flow. Take advantage of this and make sure during hot summer months blades are spinning counterclockwise, which will push air down and create a cool breeze and help to keep the room a more even temperature. In colder months you should set the blades to spin clockwise to draw air up, which will help redistribute the warm, heated air. The blade direction switch is located on the outside of the ceiling fan mount housing.

# CHAPTER 6

## The Bedroom (Not the Laundromat!)

---

### Supplies Needed

- ❏ 4–5 large boxes or bins with lids for storage
- ❏ 3–5 boxes for sorting
- ❏ 1 donation box
- ❏ Masking tape
- ❏ Marker
- ❏ Pen and paper
- ❏ Trash bags
- ❏ Laundry detergent
- ❏ Hamper
- ❏ Small bucket with warm, soapy water
- ❏ Washcloth
- ❏ Vacuum

*Y*our bedroom should primarily function as a place of relaxation. Whether you have your own or share it with a partner or roommate, your bedroom should be a spot for you to relax and unwind after a long day. Unfortunately, all too often, the surfaces in our bedrooms can quickly turn into depositories for dirty laundry and piles of junk. And for some, the mere thought of making the bed every day is overwhelming. In this chapter, I'll help you declutter your bedroom and give you valuable shortcuts that will make keeping your space tidy easy and fun!

### Wading through Your Clean Clothes

Laundry is one of the toughest tasks to manage and keep under control. Sorting through it sucks up a tremendous amount of time, and it makes your room and life more disorganized. My goal is to help you save time, be able to get dressed quickly, and keep your room looking great! We'll start by gathering all of your clean clothes. If you're lucky enough to have a dedicated laundry area in your home, it's possible there are clean clothes piled up there, possibly folded but probably just thrown into a hamper as you emptied the dryer to make room for more. If you don't have a laundry room, most of your laundry pileups will probably occur in the bedroom. Wherever it tends to pile up for you, be sure and get *all* of the clean laundry. We're going to be taking it to the bedroom!

It's time to finally put that clean laundry away. If you have lots of clean laundry to put away, we are going to make room in your dresser for what you are actually wearing first! Grab around four or five large boxes that aren't too big and have lids, as well as some masking tape and a marker to temporarily label them. Mark them with types of clothing that you own a lot of, which deserve their own category, like shirts, pants, dresses, socks/underwear, season that's ending like winter or summer, anything that makes up a noteworthy category for you, as well as one for donations. Some people have as few as three, and some people will have more than five, but if you've been following the chapters in order, you should have enough boxes you can reuse for this room. You can move these sort-box contents into the storage boxes with lids after you have put away things you are wearing, and then more easily stack them. If you don't go back into the container in a year, consider donating those contents as well. **TIP: If you have a particularly nice suit or dress you plan on wearing more than once, invest in a garment bag to keep it looking nice and protect it, rather than throwing it into a box with everything else.**

The first thing I want you to realize is that if your closet and dresser drawers are full and you're still living out of your hamper, then 90 percent of what you currently have in your dresser and closet are things you are *not* actively wearing. If you have filled these things with non-clothing items and there is no room for clothing storage, it's time to reassess what lives in your dresser or wardrobe. Whatever the case may be, I advise you to clear out enough closet or dresser space to have at least half of it dedicated to clothes.

If you have a dresser and it's already stuffed full of clothes, take the time to empty it and sort the contents into the boxes of what you're not wearing by category. Work one drawer at a time to evaluate if you wear each item or not. If you are regularly using that dresser drawer, is there anything in there that you haven't worn in six months or is out of season? **TIP: It will do you no good if out-of-season clothing is mixed in with seasonal clothing.**

Keep in mind that how you fold determines how much space is taken up. While you can often fit a lot in a dresser drawer, if you cannot see what you have, it does you no good! For example, let's take a look at the T-shirts you've collected. If you have a ton of T-shirts in one drawer, first separate what you don't wear and put them in a box, and then roll up the others that you do wear to fit neatly in the drawer, perhaps with the front design visible so you can easily grab which one you want. The same goes for hoodies.

Pants, I'd fold and stack like a display at the store or hang them in the closet. That is a personal preference; do what works best for you.

After the dresser is complete, do the same thing with the closet. I would have a separate box for shoes that you aren't wearing every day or that are for another season. Again, out-of-season clothing should be removed where possible and go in its own area for storage, preferably one that is not "prime real estate" in your main closet. Winter outerwear, which tends to be very bulky and take up a lot of space, should be moved to a separate closet when possible or off to one side of your closet and out of the way.

---

| SHOULD IT STAY OR SHOULD IT GO? | You may wonder, *is it really worth storing and having all this excess*? The answer is, maybe not. Keep in mind: long–term storage |

in cardboard may not be the best idea. Bugs can get into cardboard, and if a box gets wet, it can ruin your clothes, so be careful where you store boxes of items you're not using, or opt for a plastic storage bin with a lid. If you find you need more than five boxes, please take another hard look at your wardrobe: Do you actually wear the clothes? Love the clothes? Are you comfortable in the clothes? Do the clothes fit? If you answer no to these questions, consider donating, selling, or throwing them in the trash if they are in need of repairs.

---

Once everything is divided up, you can decide how much of it you would like to keep hanging in your closet or folded in your dresser. I like to hang work shirts and pants in the closet, so I can easily and quickly get dressed for work. I keep the casualwear folded in the dresser, but it's up to you. You know what's best for your lifestyle. Put anything you haven't worn in a very long time into a box or bag to donate or give away. Just remember that as long as you keep about three inches or more of space to slide your hangers around in your closet, you'll have a much easier time when you go to your clothes. I love the way hangers look when they all match in the closet. They take up a lot less room when they are all the same, and it makes everything look so organized!

Now, tape the sheet of paper to the inside of your closet. Note which boxes you're storing inside the closet and what's inside them, so you will know exactly what's in there and will be able to get to it easily when you want to. Stack the boxes in the back of your closet, in a spot where they are out of your way, but you can get to them if you need them. Keep the shoes you wear regularly—three or four pairs maximum—at the foot of your closet or in a shoe rack. If you want to keep the floor clear, use one of those hanging shoe organizers. Take your donation bag and put it in your car for the next time you go out. **TIP: Try this system out for a few weeks. If you find you never go into the boxes you have filled and labeled and stacked in your closet even though they're in season, consider donating them as well. It means more free space for you!**

### Cleaning Up the Dirty Laundry

New rule: dirty clothes should not be littered around your room. Put them in a hamper. Choose a nice one that goes with the décor in your room. If you're not sure whether an item is dirty or clean, better safe than sorry: assume it's dirty. You may be able to get two wears out of some items before laundering them; if you intend to wear something twice, after wearing it the first time, hang it up inside out so you know it's been worn once already. Wash it after you wear it twice—no exceptions.

*Everything needs a home that makes sense, so store things where they will be used as best you can and always put things away when you're done with them.*

If you are lucky enough to have a washer and dryer in your home, grab that hamper and go! Start a load directly from your full hamper. **TIP: Mesh lingerie bags are inexpensive. Place undergarments and socks in separate bags to protect them and** make it easier to put away when the laundry is clean and dry. No more lost socks! I cannot stress this tip enough; it is a game changer. It will also be easier and faster to keep your laundry separate from other roommates or family members. It is faster to put everything away when it all goes into the same room, closet, or dresser.

Once you pull them from the dryer, clothes should be folded and/or put away immediately. When you let them sit in the dryer until they cool, they get wrinkled, and then you'll have to iron them. Get your most wrinkle-prone clothes on hangers as soon as possible. **TIP: Allow materials that pill easily to air-dry in your shower. Putting them in a dryer causes them to pill and become less comfortable and attractive.**

If you don't have a washer and dryer in the house, the same basic rules apply; you just have the added step of transporting the laundry. Be sure you have a laundry bag or basket that will hold the shape of folded laundry, or you'll be dealing with masses of wrinkles. Put away items when you return to your home—in incremental handfuls if need be—and never go to bed with clean laundry in the basket. **TIP: After you put your clean clothes away, pick out your outfit for the next day. You will be amazed at how quickly you can get ready for your day by implementing this one simple step.**

Commit to putting the laundry away after each load or each trip to the laundromat. If not, you'll just wind up with a mess again. If it makes things more manageable for you to wash, dry, and put away smaller loads, try that. <u>But put your clothes away every time—no matter what!</u> It's a habit muscle you can and should build to help have a less stressful and more sanitary place to live in. And clothes are expensive; take care of the financial investment you've made in them so they can better serve you and last longer. You deserve nice things!

## Making the Bed

For some people, making the bed can be like major morning chore. It doesn't have to be this way! The less there is on your bed, the easier it is to make. Period. Pillows and comforters can really pull the look of a bedroom to a whole new adult level, but a ton of pillows can be a hassle and just get in the way when you make your bed. Keep your bedding simple so you will make it. **TIP: When you buy a comforter set, if you have a full bed or larger, get the next size up instead of just getting what matches your mattress size. The extra length looks great and covers much of the space where you can see under the bed.** If you use a twin bed, you should stick with twin-sized blankets, because anything larger is going to be much too long. Just like with pillows, the fewer blankets you have on your bed, the easier it will be to make.

You can save so much time making the bed in the morning by only having a fitted sheet on your bed and using a duvet cover. If you have never used a duvet cover, you may want to invest in one if you absolutely hate making your bed. Think of a duvet cover as a pillowcase for your blanket. Using the duvet cover will save you time daily when making the bed by eliminating the need for the traditional top sheet. If you go this route, I recommend you buy easy-to-use clips that are made especially for duvet covers to keep corners and around the perimeter of the blanket in place. It's up to you if this swap of a duvet cover for a top sheet saves you time and is easier. I recommend you try it if making your bed is something you cannot seem to accomplish, because when your bed is made, your room looks finished and amazing!

If you're wondering what to do with the top sheet that you no longer need, put it between the box spring and top mattress as a makeshift straight, non-ruffled bed skirt. Remember the real advantage of a duvet cover is that the daily task of making the bed is easier and faster—so it gets done.

The easiest fitted sheet made is the kind that has elastic that goes along the perimeter the whole way around the mattress rather than just on the corners. This type of perimeter-elastic fitted sheet prevents the sheet from popping out of place in the middle of the night and keeps it snug in place where you want it to stay. Switching to a full-elastic fitted sheet is another versatile and reliable time-saving tip when it comes to making the bed.

*Mite-y* **ANNOYING** Dust mites aren't a sign of sloppy upkeep and exist in most mattresses no matter how good you are at taking care of them; they're just a part of being a human living in a home. You can cut back on dust mites by stripping your bed, sprinkling baking soda onto the mattress, letting it sit for fifteen to twenty minutes, and then vacuuming up the baking soda. It's a good idea to try this if you're suffering from mystery allergies in the morning. Also changing those pillowcases weekly will be a big help. If your allergies continue to be or are a daily problem, consider investing in a mattress pad covering made just for this (they don't need to be laundered all the time) and you can buy allergen covers for your pillows as well. I like to just buy new pillows at least once a year when they are on sale.

I recommend changing your sheets every two weeks and keeping two sets so you can make the bed immediately and don't have to wait on the laundry to be finished. I do this, but I wash the pillowcases every week! If you don't have two sets of sheets yet, now's the time to treat yourself to a really nice, soft, luxurious set of sheets. They are amazing, and you deserve it!

## The Deep Clean

You may want to leave this step for another day, because getting laundry under control as well as organizing your dresser drawers and closets is plenty of work for one day! That being said, the next step in a fabulous bedroom is to clear all your surfaces and sort the items in your boxes.

Remove any pictures from the walls and clean them with a damp (not soggy) washcloth to get all the dust off of everything. When everything has been put into boxes, take this time to evaluate the artwork you have and what you normally keep on the surfaces. Is there anything you don't use a lot that could be put away somewhere or thrown out? Does anything belong in a different room altogether? Is there anything you've borrowed and need to return to its original owner? Is this a good time to repaint your room or pick a new, more restful color scheme? Do you need to install more shelving?

Once you have answered those questions, it's time to do a top-to-bottom deep clean. Clean all your surfaces and be sure to give the windows a good wipe while you're at it. You can use commercial cleaners for most things, but I recommend using soap and water for any mirrors. (Like we discussed back when we cleaned the bathroom, mirrors can get ruined if any ammonia gets around the edges of the mirror.)

Clean off the baseboards if you can move any larger furniture items away from the walls. Baseboards rarely get cleaned, but they look so good when they do! You might need to pull out the vacuum because the dust bunnies underneath your furniture may have grown to the size of a herd of dust elephants! **TIP: A lot of people neglect to use open wall space and keep everything on the floor, but making smart use of your vertical space is key, especially if you have high ceilings. If you own your property, all the better. Using your wall space as storage potential keeps more things off the ground for when you go to vacuum too.**

Save the vacuuming for last, because as you've cleaned and worked your way around the room, dust will fall and gather on the floor. For general upkeep, if you have a carpet in your room, you should vacuum it weekly, and don't forget under the bed!

Once your deep clean is complete, it's time to organize your stuff. Keep the clutter on your surfaces, like dressers, to an absolute minimum, and opt to store most of your things in drawers or other places where they'll be kept out of sight. This makes dusting and wiping down surfaces a lot easier moving forward. If you can get dividers to put inside your dressers to make organizing your drawers even easier, all the better, and if you're particularly handy, you might even be able to make these yourself!

### Decorating the Space

Bedrooms tend to be smaller rooms, so make sure the position of your furniture is making the most of your space. Remember, any furniture lifted off the floor with legs always makes the space look larger because your eye sees more square footage, which is helpful in a tiny space.

If you don't sleep with a partner, consider sleeping in a twin bed—it can free up a lot of space in your room for other things. You can even opt for a loft bed to maximize your floor space. Having a lofted bed makes it a little easier to get away with not making your bed in the morning, because you aren't directly looking at it. Still, making your bed in the morning will give you a clean, tidy space for yourself to come home to at night.

If you're looking to give your bedroom a whole new aesthetic, find a bed covering you like and pull the colors for any curtains or artwork from there. Maybe you have a favorite picture from a vacation or a special day that you'd like to blow up and put on your wall. When you choose a frame and mat for this picture, keep in mind the color you want your room to be and make sure it fits with the scheme. Choose a calm, restful color for your walls if you're allowed to paint them. I like a solid color that isn't too busy. You can even add a plant if you have the space!

Whether you decide to give your room a total makeover now, or just a deep clean, make sure it's calm and that the things you choose to keep in it genuinely make you happy. You want this to be a restful place you can return to again and again to wind down and relax.

---

### Bonus Tips & Tricks

❑ If your closets are overflowing, you have too much stuff. Donate, sell, or throw out what you really don't need, *especially* if it's damaged or doesn't fit, and you're waiting to fix it or lose a few pounds. Do yourself a favor and get rid of it.

❑ Have roommates? Designate a separate day for each person to do his or her laundry. Not mixing laundry makes putting it away much easier and faster.

❑ I don't like hanging laundry outside to dry, but I do love bed linens dried on the clothesline. For me, it's worth the effort—they smell so fresh and clean.

# CHAPTER 7

## The Kitchen

---

### Supplies Needed

- ❑ 3–4 sorting boxes
- ❑ Antibacterial cleaner
- ❑ Dish detergent and sponge
- ❑ Broom, dust pan, or vacuum
- ❑ Mop and soapy water
- ❑ Washcloth and dry towel
- ❑ Cooler, optional
- ❑ Hair dryer, optional

---

By far, one of the most intimidating areas to clean in any space is the kitchen. You should consider taking your time and splitting the tasks for this area over the week so you are not overwhelmed and not spending hours doing this all at once. There's something about the kitchen that naturally attracts dirt and grime; it tends to be far less contained than a bathroom, and it's typically used daily. The act of cooking in and of itself often tends to be tiresome, which makes the thought of wiping down countertops and doing dishes immediately after food prep sound downright exhausting, but getting into the habit of completing the cleanup as you use various utensils is vital to having a clean kitchen at all. This is one area that pays you back tenfold when you get and keep it clean and clear! You really do want to wake up to a sparkling clean kitchen and home; it's the best way to start any day and enjoy your morning coffee or tea.

### Never Leave Dirty Dishes in the Sink Unless You Want Roaches and Mice as Houseguests!

As you can see, I am very passionate about washing dishes immediately after using them. That's because I've seen it more times than I care to disclose: a sink filled with dirty dishes, piled up throughout the day just soaking in soapy water and waiting to be washed. This is a major mistake that can potentially open the floodgates to a costly pest infestation! If you have dirty dishes sitting out on countertops for hours, that's even worse, but just soaking a dish does not help the situation very much. It always looks sloppy, and cleaning in a crowded sink basin is much more time-consuming than cleaning in an empty one. If you live with roommates, and each person is in charge of doing their own dishes, a full sink can make cohabitation a nightmare. There is an easy way to prevent this from happening. Whenever you're done with a dish, scrape any larger chunks of food into the trash, take your dish to the sink, and wash it with dish detergent, making sure to get all sides of each dish, even the ones that might not have touched any food. You'd be surprised what can wind up on the bottom of a plate. Remember to wash your eating utensils as well, and wash the handles on all of them too, not just the utility ends! Use the hottest water possible; hot water is best for killing germs. If it's too hot to touch, rubber gloves are a lifesaver. Immediately move the dish from the sink to the drying rack once it's been washed. Your dish is now clean, and the sink is empty, so the next time you have to use it, you don't have to worry about what's inside it. Now get everyone on board to do the same!

If something is just caked onto a pot or pan and you find yourself absolutely needing to soak it in soapy water, be careful not to let it sit too long. And don't ever drop a sharp knife into soapy water, unless you like trips to the emergency room! Knives and other sharp utensils should always be washed immediately and safely stored in the drying rack. My preference is to immediately clean and dry sharp knives and place them back into the butcher block. It's the best practice for safety, especially if you have multiple cooks in the house, plus it really is very easy: rinse knife, grab dishtowel, put knife into butcher block. Simple.

If you own a dishwasher, soak pans in soapy water beforehand, and give everything a good rinse before putting them in. When you remove them from the dishwasher, make sure to examine your dishes and utensils for any residue. But if your living situation is more "every man for himself," I prefer to wash everything by hand. That way, I can be absolutely sure I'm not leaving any food behind.

Be sure and replace sponges often. Weekly is ideal; just buy a bulk pack of them and go. Don't let them get to the point where they physically look ragged before swapping them. By the time they get to this point, they're absolutely teeming with bacteria. Alternatively, ditch the sponge altogether and use a rag, which you can toss into the wash when it starts to look dirty. **TIP: If it smells, it is riddled with bacteria! Sanitize your sponge daily by filling a bowl with water, put the sponge in the water, and microwave for ninety seconds. Let it cool in the sink.**

If you don't have the time to dry dishes manually as they make their way into the dish rack, come back after they've had a few hours to drip dry so it isn't full all day. It's best to dry utensils immediately and manually, because those utensil containers you tend to find in most drying racks aren't the most sanitary of places, and definitely aren't easy to clean. Be sure to clean the drip tray every two or three weeks too. It can get pretty gross if you just let it go. Get into the habit of looking at it once in a while.

## Form Over Function—The Surfaces

A kitchen is an area that should be based around utility. Kitchens exist for the purpose of food preparation. Sometimes, a kitchen will double as the primary dining area, but either way, it's best to keep everything simple and focused so you can easily clean it every time you use it.

Keep your counters, windowsills, and the tops of cabinets and refrigerator free of knickknacks and extras. These things clutter up the room visually, and it's all too easy to spatter food particles as you cook. You'll find that grease tends to build up quickly and relentlessly—it's exactly like toilet flushes spraying bacteria everywhere in your bathroom—so the easier it is to wipe down the counter and stovetop, the better. Keep as many appliances as possible stored away in drawers or cabinets so you don't have to wipe them down constantly. Anything you use daily, like a coffeepot or sugar bowl, can be left on the counter, but keep it as far away from the stovetop as you can.

Over years of experience, I have grown to greatly dislike refrigerator magnets. It's fine to have maybe one or two to hold shopping lists and pictures you genuinely love, but anything more than three is clutter. Keeping that space empty is easier on the eyes. There are better spots in your house to keep your favorite photographs, where they aren't constantly at risk of being ruined by exposure to heat and moisture. A magnetic grocery list and a pen, however, are great to have on the fridge, especially if you share your home with others. If something runs out, it's very easy to just add it to the list when you find out you need it. If you like motivational sticky notes, you might want to try putting one inside the refrigerator where the food is for a nice surprise when you go to eat!

### Deep-Cleaning the Appliances

It may take a full day to clean inside the oven, microwave, refrigerator, and freezer because they are the hardest. You can divide it up and just tackle one a day, or even break it down by refrigerator shelf. Just keep going until it's done.

For the fridge and freezer, you'll have to work quickly as you clean, because food that needs to be kept frozen is at risk of thawing out, and food that needs to stay cool is at risk of going bad. Throw away anything that's past its expiration date right away, as well as anything that's starting to look or smell bad. **TIP: If you own a cooler, use that to store your good food while you clean to buy yourself more time. This will also keep your food away from any pets that might take a bite while you aren't paying attention.** Empty everything and scrub down the inside surfaces with a warm, soapy washcloth. Be sure to get in all the nooks and crannies, and remove any drawers so you can get everything. You can wipe it dry with a towel.

If your freezer has a lot of ice buildup on its surfaces, you're going to want to melt the ice. A lot of freezers will tackle ice deposits manually, but if yours is older, you may have to defrost it. A hair dryer can expedite the process, but make sure to sop up the water with a towel and don't let the hair dryer get wet or overheated. Be sure and wipe everything down when it's dry.

Label all food that goes into your freezer with a date and its contents. I don't keep meats in the freezer any longer than six months, and I put newer stuff in the back and toward the bottom, so I am always using the oldest product first: the last in, first out rule. That gives it less time to accumulate freezer damage, which ruins the taste. Make sure all containers are sealed to avoid icy buildup, and place similar items together to make meal planning easy.

---

ON THE *Cold Front* To keep tabs on how well your freezer is freezing things, keep a clear plastic bottle filled about halfway with water in your freezer. Wait for it to freeze completely, then drop a dime inside and leave the bottle in your freezer. If for any reason that dime winds up inside the block of ice instead of on top of it, then your freezer isn't freezing foods properly, and you should think about replacing or repairing it if you haven't recently had a power outage. And if you have, it'll let you know if the power outage lasted long enough to possibly defrost your food.

---

In the fridge, keep raw meat on the lowest shelf so that if it leaks, it has less potential to contaminate your other food. Breakfast foods and vegetables should be placed in groups so you can easily see if you're running out and don't have to go looking for things when you plan your meals. A lot of refrigerators come with a dedicated vegetable drawer so your veggies are stored in the optimal temperature. If your fridge runs cold, you don't want to stick your leafy greens near the back where they can freeze!

Condiments have a tendency to accumulate in the refrigerator doors; aim for only one container per condiment that you use regularly. If you have multiple ketchups or jars of mayonnaise or bottles of barbecue sauce, see if you can consolidate them to free up space. When the whole unit is back in order, give it a good scrubbing on all sides, including on top. You'd be surprised how much dust can collect on top of the fridge.

The microwave is comparatively easier to clean than the fridge due to its size. Clean the microwave by heating a mug of water for two minutes and keep it in the microwave for an additional five minutes. The steam condensation on the inside will have helped to loosen any crud and make wiping it out much easier. Don't forget to clean the outside of the microwave, too, especially if it's close enough to the stove that grease can build up on the outside. The buttons and handle are prone to getting dirty quickly.

Last are the stove and oven. Do yourself a favor and purchase a good oven-cleaner product that is fume-free. Those cleansers are especially good for dirty drip pans, which you can access by opening the stove top. **TIP: You can use the bottom drawer for bakeware storage. For easier cleanups, I keep a piece of aluminum foil on the bottom of my oven just in case something drips out of a baking dish.**

Stovetops are important to clean <u>every time</u> you use them. Make sure your stovetop is cool before you start to clean it! I have an electric, flat-top range because it's the easiest to wipe down. However, not everybody has one of those. With gas ranges, you're going to have to wipe underneath the burner grates, because it's all too easy to get dirt trapped under them. The first time you give those burner grates a deep clean, they may be the exception to the "don't spend too much time soaking things in the sink" rule, just due to the sheer amount of food that's probably been caked on them during your stovetop's lifetime. The first time is always the hardest, but it gets easier if you keep up with it. I'd soak them in a solution of water and dish detergent to get them to a presentable state. But ultimately, a stovetop is one of those things that can go from sparkling clean to a disaster zone in a snap if you're not diligent about cleaning it up.

Don't forget to wipe off the knobs on your oven and stove, as well as the oven handle. You'd be amazed at how much greasy buildup can accumulate on those little knobs. If yours are removable, you can soak them along with the burner grates.

### Organize Your Storage Space for Maximum Efficiency

Now that the appliances are clean and gleaming, you're going to want to reorganize your cabinets too. As with everything else you've cleaned so far, you're going to empty your cabinets and drawers and sort the contents into boxes, grouping like items together. Throw away any items that are expired or broken—no exceptions.

Consider doing one or two cabinets at a time to keep this to a manageable amount and not a marathon. Perhaps start with one or two kitchen drawers, or one drawer each day till the job is done. Start with the one most used. Nothing has to be perfect, but if it's hard to get a utensil when you need it or it looks dirty, you need to dig in and get it done.

Once empty, give the cabinets a thorough scrubbing with soap and water, inside and out. If you notice any dead insects or rodent droppings inside drawers take them out and clean completely.

When your drawer or cabinet is good and clean, start putting things back in, taking care to keep things lined up in an orderly fashion. It helps sometimes to get minishelves so you can stack smaller containers and save space. If you don't already have a spice rack, having one that fits inside your cabinets comfortably is a game changer. I wouldn't spend significant money on new storage containers or shelving units, but I have found that lazy Susans are particularly handy for storing spices.

Remember, this is about clearing out what you don't use and organizing what you do need in a place that makes sense according to how often you need it and what it's used for. Look for any chipped dishes or utensils you aren't using, and get rid of them. Additionally, after throwing away any expired or dubious food items, you should have a lot more space in your cabinets than you did before. Can you free up an entire cabinet to store some of your less-frequently-used small appliances instead of putting them on top of the fridge or on the counter? You want to have as much counter surface to work with as possible in your kitchen while you're cooking. Plus, you don't have to spend as much time cleaning appliances that are stored away in a cabinet! Try to keep heavy items closer to the ground and lighter items higher up, because the bigger they are, the harder they fall. If you need to get a small stepladder to reach the highest shelves, by all means, do so. Keep it out of the way until you need to use it—safety first!

If you have a lot of cookbooks, these are great to keep in cabinets. Leaving them out on the counter all the time is a good way to get them dirty. It may be a good idea to keep only your favorite recipes on hand in a binder rather than keeping a stack of cookbooks where you only use a small percentage of the recipes inside them. They can pile up fast if you aren't careful, so when you try a recipe, be honest about what you think of it. Sticky notes in your cookbooks are amazing for keeping track of this, and they can also help if you want to modify a recipe. If you find that you've tried everything in a cookbook and really only like one or two recipes, make a copy of the ones you want and put them in a recipe binder, and then donate the cookbook, so it isn't taking up so much space.

Plastic containers will likely require a full drawer or shelf on their own. They accumulate quickly. Have a few designated red-sauce containers, because we've all seen how they get after you store red sauce in it just once. I'd make sure at least one of your red-sauce containers is large enough to accommodate a full recipe. Get rid of all the containers without any lids and any peeling ones. Ideally, replace your plastic collection with glass containers that have removable vented lids for microwave reheats. These will last longer, and the glass will not stain.

You probably have a cabinet under your kitchen sink as well. I recommend only storing your cleaners here. Clean it out and scrub it down like the other cabinets, checking for cracks where pests might be able to come in. If you have pets or small children that you wouldn't want getting into your cleaning supplies, it can be good to install locks in this area. **TIP: I keep my cleaners in a plastic** basket so I can pull the whole thing out at once. I also buy the smaller size, so the product gets used up and doesn't take up a lot of space.

If your silverware drawer doesn't have a divider inside, now is the time to get one. It keeps your silverware separated and easily accessible. Take inventory of what tools you have, and remember to toss or donate duplicates and ones you really don't love or use.

If you typically keep a roll of paper towels on a vertical rack on your countertop, I strongly suggest investing in a horizontal one you can mount underneath a cabinet—just not the one directly above the stovetop; that is a fire waiting to happen! I like to have it underneath the cupboards so it isn't taking up counter space. I am not a fan of keeping a crock with stove utensils on the counter either. It looks messy and takes up valuable space. If you can, ditch this item and keep those utensils in a drawer close to the stove. Also, keep your spoon rest in the drawer, too, and you can pull it out to the countertop to use when cooking if you need to.

## Trash Management

A lot of homes have dedicated drawers to keep trash bags out of sight and out of mind. Depending on how large your household is and how much trash it generates, this may not be enough, but I do like to keep trash in a discreet location. If you can get one of those trash cans with the foot pedal, so you aren't touching the bin very often, that's always a good idea, but I especially like it when a piece of furniture can conceal a trash bag entirely.

Take the trash out as soon as the bag starts to look full. It stinks, and if you try to cram as much of it into one bag as you can, the underside of the trash can lid will get dirty very fast. **TIP: Grab the trash from the bathroom and other rooms as well at least once a week. It's a good idea to get into the habit of physically cleaning your trash cans about once every other week.**

I like to put a drop of essential oil on a paper towel and drop it into the bottom of a trash can to cut back on odors. If you collect disposable grocery bags from the store to reuse as garbage bags, it's good to have a container to keep them in—perhaps mounted to a wall or stored in a cabinet—so you can access them easily. They make very good liners for smaller trash cans, like the ones in your bathrooms or office. Never, ever use a trash can without lining it with a bag, because your trash can will get dirty, and that's another really good way to get bugs in your house! Using the liner keeps you from having to clean the can again and again.

### The Floors

Cleaning the floors and baseboards is always a pain, but something you will need to do it periodically. I vacuum my kitchen floor multiple times during the week, and I suggest you do too—at least once a week. I use the wand attachment to get the baseboards and all those hard-to-reach spaces. Try it and see if this makes it easier for you to keep the floors clean. If you have pets, do this every other day. You will want to clean your floors once a month with soap and water or at least when they start to look dirty, and definitely once a month with soap and water if you have pets.

### Decorating the Space

If you want to add a plant to the kitchen, a nice option is to go for a windowsill herb garden. Cilantro, chives, parsley, and thyme have all worked well for me in this regard. If you live in a warmer climate, cilantro has a tendency to bolt and go to seed if it gets particularly hot, so be proactive about swapping out your plants regularly, and don't be afraid to prune them, or they'll generally have a shorter lifespan. Basil has been more of a success for me outdoors because of how big it can get if you're diligent about pruning it. Basil plants need to be pruned particularly aggressively because they go to seed quickly.

I suggest you add a custom soap dispenser to the kitchen sink area for dishwashing detergent if you don't have a built-in dispenser unit attached to your sink. A soap dispenser on the counter has a more finished and intentional look than the store packaged liquid dishwashing soap bottles. Plus, you can buy it in a larger, more economical size, saving over time. The bottle should be stored close at hand under the sink, that way it's out of sight. With the dispenser I have, there is the added convenience of easily squirting a few pumps on the sponge without having to pick up the detergent bottle. My kitchen sink looks nicer with soap in a pump dispenser, and washing my hands or dishes is easier.

Kitchen knobs and pulls are easy to replace and can make a huge visual difference. Cost can vary, and this can potentially get pretty pricey depending on your taste and the quantity needed. But there are many different price points out there! If you're renting and want to swap out your kitchen handles, just keep the old ones in a baggie to swap back should you move out.

Battery-operated sensor lighting can be mounted under your kitchen cabinets. Just be sure to get the small ones and mount them toward the front, so you don't see them. They even make battery-operated lighting with a remote.

A small rug looks really nice in front of the sink, and if you have a tile floor in your kitchen, you will be more comfortable with a rug. Go a little oversized for the rug in this space.

## Bonus Tips & Tricks

❑ Date and mark anything that goes into the freezer so you know what it is and how long it's been in there. You can do this in the fridge too, on products like mayonnaise and leftovers. I use painter's tape and a permanent marker pen.

❑ For a more satisfying dining experience, eat sitting down at the dining room or kitchen table. You can even light a candle at dinner to make it special. Just don't forget to blow it out when you get up!

# CHAPTER 8

## Your Home Office

---

### Supplies Needed

- ☐ Microfiber duster
- ☐ Compressed air canister
- ☐ Banker Box
- ☐ File folders
- ☐ Trash bag
- ☐ Shred bag
- ☐ Small box
- ☐ Spiral notebook
- ☐ Calendar with monthly and weekly at-a-glance sections
- ☐ Wall calendar, optional

---

*W*hile not everyone has a room for a dedicated home office, most households do have a workspace where papers are filed, bills are paid, letters are stamped, or at the very least, where a computer lives. It might be a section of the living room or your bedroom, or it might be somewhere else entirely. Wherever it is for you, I'm here to help you make yours a productive one!

If you haven't yet moved to electronic statements and payments and are still using paper, below you will find some best practices in organizing yourself and your paperwork. If you have transitioned to electronic payments or are ready to do so, that will be covered more in the Computer Organization section.

### All the Paper, Paper, Paper

Keep your files and bills together and use a month-at-a-glance planner or an electric planner or calendar to make sure you pay those bills on time. Consider setting up auto pay where you can.

You will need some file folders and a box of some sort to keep all of your papers together. I like to use hanging file folders and a dedicated filing cabinet, just because it keeps the paperwork out of the way. You can raid the back-to-school section at your local retailer when school and office supplies go on sale to save on these items. Group your folders by color, which can make things easy to pick up at a glance, and store them handily in a banker box if you don't have a filing cabinet. I suggest the following categories for file folders:

- BILLS FOLDER. I keep this one up front and also mark my paper calendar with due dates. (You can and should just as easily mark your electronic calendar/planner if you don't use a paper one.) You can throw any paper receipts in this folder, so it's easy to reconcile the credit card bill, for example, when it comes in. Once you have everything reconciled at the end of the month, you can discard the receipts unless you need to keep them for tax purposes. If this is the case, you can then move the papers to a TAXES folder and mark the tax year on the tab as well. This way you have everything in one place at the end of the year. If you're running a business out of your home, you can (and should) have separate business folders for bills you need to pay and invoices you need to collect on.

 I have a spot in my planner to write when all my bills are due, including those with scheduled auto payments. I pay all my bills that are due on or before the eighteenth on the first of the month, then pay all the ones that are due the eighteenth or after on the fifteenth of the month. To save myself more time and earn some benefits, I have set up many of the bills, like my insurance and phone bill, to be automatically charged to a credit card each month so that I can receive points at no additional charge to me. If I cannot pay via a credit card, then I set the bill up to be paid from my checking account. I balance my checkbook in the middle of the month with the second round of bill paying. It takes me less than two hours for the month and avoids those nasty late payments. For more, see chapter 9's Bill Payments.

- PENDING ORDERS FOLDER. If you have a business you're running and ship items frequently, this is a very useful folder to have up front or close to it. It is also useful for notes on any online orders or returns you have placed. You can reconcile this at the end of each month when you pay your bills and balance your checkbook.
- STATIONERY, CARDS, AND STAMPS FOLDER. Historically, I kept this folder next because I used it a lot. However, I have found it's easier for me to have a separate decorative box for this.

The rest of my folders, I like to sort alphabetically. These are the ones I use, but feel free to add your own as you see fit. (I keep the

BILLS and PENDING up front because it's fastest and easiest for me to retrieve that way.)

- AUTO
- BANKING
- BILLS
- CLIENTS
- CREDIT CARDS. If you have more than one, put them in alphabetical order within the folder. Pay these suckers off each month! It's not a sale if you can't pay it off when the bill comes in.
- IMPORTANT DOCUMENTS. Passports, birth certificates, driver's license copies, vehicle registration slips, etc. You may want to keep these in a separate closed file folder in a small fireproof safe or in a safety deposit box at your bank. Most banks will offer this for free.
- MEDICAL
- PROJECTS. For short- or long-term project ideas that you want to do, include information as well as scheduling steps needed and be sure to mark a month to start the project or a reminder in your planner or e-calendar.
- RENT & UTILITY AGREEMENTS. I keep these all in the one folder, especially if I'm in an apartment.
- TAX RETURNS
- WARRANTIES & MANUALS
- WILLS. If you don't have one, get one. This is something everyone needs, and you can easily and inexpensively set this up. Just get it notarized and witnessed by someone other than the executors or any beneficiaries.

You can add any folders you want, but keeping them alphabetized keeps everything simple and easy to access. You do not need a ton of folders and individual files; combine files that make sense. For example, HEALTH can include dental as well as all other doctor visits and blood work rather than three separate files for each subcategory. You can make a HOME file to include your rent, home insurance, electric/gas/water/cable bills, and furniture purchases. Feel free to personalize your files as needed!

### Computer Organization

If you can manage your paper files, then managing your computer files will be a piece of cake. They are very similar. First, create umbrella folders for WORK, HOME, and any other aspects (project or topic) of your life that have the potential for a lot of paperwork and/or information. Then create subfolders within those folders. Using the example from above, you may have a HOME folder that holds folders each for ELECTRIC, GAS, WATER, and CABLE. Perhaps in HOME, there is also a COLLEGE file that holds student loan information. Maybe you have a PERSONAL folder in HOME that houses photos and downloads. Remember, your desktop can get visually cluttered very fast. Be sure to make enough "umbrella" folders to drag, for instance, all eight hundred kitchen remodeling images into the HOME/KITCHEN REMODEL folder.

### Email

Email can be very hard to keep up with. You can sort messages by unread, you can star or color flag the important ones, and create folders just like you did for your desktop. Create a few folders if you really want to keep old emails or if you need them for work; just get them out of your inbox if you've answered them. If you are waiting for a reply or information, it can get a little tricky. You don't want to forget about the email, but it can get in the way of keeping your inbox organized. You can make a pending folder, but you have to make sure to check it. I like to keep a spiral notebook on top of my desk where I can list critical reminders, then put the email, or paper document, in an appropriate folder. **TIP: Make sure to back up your computer at least once a month to some external source.**

## Cleaning and Organizing

Whatever sort of computer you've invested in, make sure nothing is crowding it to prevent overheating. If you have something that's easy to open, such as a desktop PC, get in the habit of spraying the insides with compressed air to remove dust, or at least the exhaust ports if you're not comfortable with (or capable of) opening the machine. Dust accumulates quickly inside electronics and can cause fans to break prematurely and, in a worst-case scenario, for the machine to shut down entirely at random, costing you valuable time if you aren't in the habit of saving your progress often. Make sure the device is not on when you clean the interior, and try not to touch anything directly if you don't completely understand which parts are which. When in doubt, call in a professional, and they can walk you through the process of cleaning your machine. A good professional can do this for you, as well as help back up your files externally. I have my photos backed up in two separate locations.

You'll want to get into the habit of dusting off the surface of your electronics too, especially peripherals that aren't used very often. You probably paid a lot for them, so take good care of them. Microfiber cloths misted with a light amount of water can get most smudges off of your screens. A microfiber duster is good for the outsides, and if your keyboard is prone to getting a lot of dust and mysterious dirt particles in it, compressed air comes in handy here too. If you're ever not sure about whether a component should be touched, but you know it's dirty, compressed air is usually a safe bet; again, when in doubt, ask a professional—especially if you have a laptop that's still under warranty.

Keep cables tied together and out of the way, so you're not tripping over them, and it's important to label them. Masking tape works here, but dedicated labels specifically for cable management are a real thing now, and they can make your cable management look a lot more professional. For any random charge cords—you know the ones, the odd cords where you don't know where they came from or what device they're supposed to connect to—roll them up, secure them with a rubber band and a label (even if the label is just the type of cable), and put it in a drawer specifically for those odd cables. I've found most cables are interchangeable as long as you're using the right type, so if you can learn to identify what kind of cable you have, you can judge if it's a duplicate that can be thrown or given away, or if it's a vital component to something.

Keep all external memory storage (flash drives and hard drives, usually) in a dedicated bin in a drawer. Hard drives are much more fragile than flash drives, so store them in the lowest drawer possible to minimize the possibility of dropping them or knocking them off the desk. Make sure to back up your hard drive monthly in case of emergencies. In the event of computer failure, the first question anybody will ask you when you say your computer's dead is, "Did you back it up recently?" Make sure the answer to that question is always yes! If you haven't backed up your computer, and you don't have an external hard drive to back it up to, run down to the store and get one for the important stuff, like your documents, music, and pictures. Alternatively, you can subscribe to a cloud service that backs your computer up automatically for you. I like to save money and do it manually. Mark your calendar for this one and get someone to show you how to do this if you don't already know how!

## Decorating the Space

If you do have a dedicated area for a home office, the most important investment you can make, no matter how big or small the area is, will be your office chair. Pick something that goes with the color scheme of your room. I like to use a tan, brown, or burgundy if you're in a room with a warmer color scheme, and black for a room with a cooler color scheme. You'll be spending a lot of time in it, so don't skimp if you can help it. Make sure it fits with your desk and isn't too big or small. If you can, go to an office supply store and sit and *spend some time* in the chairs on display to get a feel for what's comfortable. Remember the ones you like, and check online to see if you can get a good deal on a nice one. Get something comfortable! You will be more likely to stay put and get your work done with a good chair.

The home office is one area where I would actually *not* encourage placing a plant. You'll have to water it, and if it spills, it could get all over your electronics and paperwork, which would be terrible. But lighting is important, especially if you have an analog workflow with real paper. A nice swivel lamp mounted on your desk will keep the eye strain away, and if there's room, a few pictures of people you love or a vacation that made you happy would be great here. If you're into vision boards or saving for a big vacation, this would be a good spot for an inspiration photo or poster. I like to put a picture of my family here too because they are very important to me. They remind me to balance my work and to schedule regular time off, even a short planned hike or packed lunch and a bike ride so that we can spend time together out in nature. You can always put a photo of the next vacation you are saving for as inspiration for when morale is low, knowing that soon you will be enjoying a wonderful adventure. Having a visual reminder helps me to make the most of each day.

Make sure the shelving on your desk works for the appliances you have. If you have a printer, have a space for it nearby, so you're not walking all the way across a room to print or scan a document. Put it on a dresser or desktop, so you don't have to crouch down to use it. Always keep your cords labeled and tidy, and put ones you're not using away in a covered box or drawer for easy access when needed. Always clean your desk off at the end of the day and put everything away. And a weekly wipe of this area goes a long way.

## Bonus Tips & Tricks

❑ Do not eat or drink while working at your computer. This will keep it clean and safe from spills and extra dirt and grime.

❑ A lot of the random cables in your home are duplicates. If you learn to identify them, you can get rid of the extras.

❑ No matter how many times you've read this chapter, you probably need to back up your computer now. You should put the book down and do that.

# CHAPTER 9

## Your Schedule

*A*nother area to reevaluate so you can get the most out of it isn't a room at all—it's your time. Evaluating how you manage your time isn't just about making sure you're optimizing your living arrangements, so you're not wasting valuable time going from room to room in a manner that doesn't make sense; it's also about buying planners and setting alarms to set a schedule that will work for you, help you use your time more efficiently, and live a life balanced with work and play and personal goal achievements. Time is the only finite resource we really have, so we need to make the best of it.

### Calendars and Logistical Scheduling

You probably have a calendar app on your phone and/or computer, but don't dismiss the idea of having a physical calendar as well! I keep a month-at-a-glance calendar on the wall in the kitchen; it is just a basic, old-fashioned paper calendar. You can probably get some free promotional calendars from businesses you frequent; these can and do work great for adding appointments and engagements.

I live by an 8" x 10" paper planner with the month and week at a glance, which makes it easy for me to schedule tasks and appointments and check my availability. I find it very useful to have the month at a glance, and the weekly time block as well, to plan my days. I usually do week planning every Sunday night and use the month as a guide to schedule tasks into the week-at-a-glance layout. I review this planner each morning to keep me on track, and then at the end of each day, I highlight my completed tasks and appointments. This has proven very helpful for me to reach my personal and profession goals.

## Bill Payments

My planner layout has room on the right side of the monthly page to list all my bills—both auto and manual pay—in separate areas as well as space for five daily entries. I typically schedule an hour to pay my bills during the week and pick a day to do so depending on what else is happening that week. I don't usually need the whole hour because most of my bills are on auto pay, but it does allow me to highlight what's been paid on my monthly calendar and add them to my bank register as the month progresses.

If you are like me and balance your checkbook, this time will also allow you to add any auto payments from your checking account to your check register and any debit card purchases or ATM withdrawals you may have made during the week. During this time, I also move any ATM or debit receipts from my wallet and add them into my check register. I save those receipts until I balance my account at the end of each month with the banking statement. If you are making a lot of debit card purchases, schedule time to do this every week instead of twice a month to stay on top of things and know exactly how much cash you have available in your checking account. It's an awful feeling when you are suddenly caught low, incur bounced check fees, or are unable to pay off your credit card and incur interest charges. As a rule, I put my debit and credit card receipts in my wallet at the time of purchase and move them to the BILLS folder as soon as I can.

### Online versus Paper

The most important thing about any calendar is to use it! Look at it at the end of each day and in the morning, so nothing gets missed. If you prefer the electronic version, that will work as long as you look at it night and day! If you are missing appointments or late paying bills, you may need a paper calendar. Pick one that you will use.

If you've tried the paper and it didn't work, try the electronic and then set the alarm or vice versa, but for either of these to work you need to develop the habit of looking at the calendar regularly before you go to bed and when you wake up in the morning for it to keep you on track.

---

ON *Track* AND
ON *Time*

I like to use a planner for work and personal goals. Some people don't find them all that helpful, but if you're one of those who absolutely needs one, welcome to the club! I keep my planner with me in my car and take it pretty much everywhere I go. Mine has a spiral binding and the month has tabs for easy access and opens up so that the month is actually two 8" x 10" pages side by side, and the one-week layout on the next pages is the same format. It makes for a lot of room to make notes, as well as room to put in a party invitation address or the invitation itself. I love picking out new designs every year, and I sprinkle some happy stickers throughout the month and weekdays to keep it looking great. Have fun choosing one with a cover that really reflects your personality, and if you can't find a cover you like, you can always decorate it yourself!

---

Online calendars are very handy if you use your computer or phone a lot, and those integrated reminder systems where you can set an alarm when an event is coming up offer an advantage: you don't have to keep the paper version with you all the time. The e-version has an additional advantage of easily sharing your calendar with anyone else you choose. Some online calendars come with label options too, so you can color-code your events. So even if you're not tech savvy, they are definitely worth looking into. (Personally, I wouldn't replace it fully with the wall calendar. There's something that's just very satisfying about having everything on the wall in a place where I can see it often.)

## Optimizing Your Workflow

Life's too short to spend it walking back and forth across a room to find something or maintaining items that bring you no joy! Keeping your belongings orderly and beautiful boils down to developing routines, putting things away immediately after you're done using them, and not having more stuff than your space allows. Know your limitations when it comes to high-maintenance décor (plants) and furniture (glass table tops). If you love an item but it requires constant cleaning and maintenance to function, it can quickly drain your energy and wind up neglected. You deserve a nice place and nice things, and your part in that is to know what you are willing and able to do to make sure your habitat is functional and presentable. You will be surprised how well you can manage with a little organization and a good, solid plan!

Think about how you navigate your home on a daily basis. Are there any instances where in order to complete a task, you're doing a lot of back-and-forth travel for something that shouldn't take that much effort? It artificially lengthens the task, which eats up time that's better spent on recreation. Consider moving things around. Maybe it's a trash can that's too far away from the sink, an herb garden that's too far from the kitchen to be functional, or a shed that's nowhere near your pool or garden. Make a mental list the next time it takes unnecessary steps or time to put something away. Figure out a way to rearrange things to make it easier to return items to their home and access items when you need them.

Also, use this time to make sure the pathways through your home are clear to navigate. Stepping around inconveniently placed furniture can be a real time waster. If you're having trouble figuring out what's working and what isn't simply due to habit, bringing in a second opinion can help a lot. Maybe have a trusted friend come by and spend a few days living in your space just to have that outside perspective. Even just having friends over for a few hours and watching them try to move about in the normal designated guest areas can tell you a lot if you take some time and observe what's going on. This is often easily noticed when cooking in a kitchen with someone else!

### Meal Planning

Meal planning is one of the hardest tasks for most people, but it doesn't have to be! Planning and organizing your meals isn't inherently difficult, but can have a tremendous positive impact on your health, day, and wallet. A small change in your daily routine and habits can have a big positive effect on your well-being.

Make a quick list of your favorite dinners, lunches, and breakfasts—now you have a basic grocery list. Keep one or two thirty-minute dinners in your tool belt and consider doubling the recipe when you cook. Leftovers can be amazing and are so handy to have! **TIP: If you save food for leftovers, make sure the containers are airtight when they go into the freezer. Freezer burn can absolutely ruin a meal you worked hard on. Label and date everything before it goes in.**

Preparing ingredients the night before and tossing them into a slow cooker before you leave the house once a week is also great for both your wallet and your morale. It may help to break out that planner or calendar and write down ideas for meals as they come to you. Buying staples like rice and beans and pasta in bulk is a good idea if you have the storage space. You can even get nice, custom containers for them, and they're very common bases for meals, so if you're genuinely stumped for options, you can make a rice or pasta base and then sauté up whatever vegetables and protein you have on hand to make a quick stir-fry and spread it out over the week.

Maybe try out an old recipe book you've had, just to see if anything in it tastes good. It can help to take notes on a recipe, but a lot of the time, if a recipe is a real keeper, you just know. If you limit the number of recipes in your repertoire to just the ones where you know immediately that you're going to want it again, having fewer options can actually make it easier to keep them *all* straight. Definitely keep a dedicated "favorites" binder for those immediate winners, and list them out somewhere in the kitchen where you can see them.

If you live with others, split up cooking chores as a matter of basic courtesy. For example, if you cook dinner, I will happily wash the dishes and clean up. If you'd rather just consolidate cooking and cleaning into blocks based on what day it is, some people work better that way. Unless someone you live with is a truly awful cook, it helps to split the workload if you're already splitting groceries. Try it for a week and see. You will save time by not having to cook and clean up every night and will hopefully spend some quality time with the people you live with.

## Bonus Tips & Tricks

❑ Life-work balance is important! Make sure all of your personal projects and/or activities also land on your calendar.

❑ The less clutter you have in your home, the easier you can clean and navigate through it, saving you time.

❑ Take notes to remember things, because nobody plans to forget them!

❑ When you're done with something, put it back immediately, so there are fewer visual distractions for you to contend with and no clean up later.

# CHAPTER 10

# *Your Outdoor Living Space(s)*

*I*ndoor living spaces often spill over into outdoor living spaces. Carve out time for yourself to utilize this oft-overlooked refuge. In other words, if you're fortunate enough to have a porch, deck, balcony, patio, yard, or any other type of space for relaxing and entertaining, enjoy it! You can create a welcoming environment by investing in a patio table and some chairs. Take some time to personalize it and make it comfortable.

## Furniture

There's a certain strategy to placing your outdoor furniture. Usually, it's best to keep chairs where people sit for an extended amount of time in the shade, but if you have a tree that drips sticky sap or sheds pollen all over, you may want to pick a different location for any tables and chairs. If you own the home, consider getting rid of that messy tree once and for all by a professional. You can install shades manually, so you don't necessarily need to have a tree around if you want shade, and not having to clean the furniture every time you want to use it makes the space a lot more inviting. Umbrellas can look nice too. Patio shade sails also look stylish, are easy to mount, and function well.

It's easier and safer to keep furniture on concrete than it is to keep it on dirt, so if what came with your property doesn't quite match the vision you have in mind, and you're allowed to do it, you can save up to get a new custom patio area put in, complete with walkways and whatever else you can imagine. Pavers can be really nice and with some research you might decide to try and update what you have with a border or outdoor rug to completely change the look. If you do decide to update a large area, be sure and plan out your yard in detail. A good idea in general is to think about a long-term plan and implement small steps each year. Remember that scale is extremely important for your space to be functional and stylish. You want a path to your seating that is easy to get to. You can mix and match materials, and by keeping the same color scheme, it will all look pulled together. Outdoor rugs have come a long way in affordability, but if mold or mildew is an issue, skip the rug. A small plant with some outdoor candles can go a long way to make your seating area more inviting and welcoming without spending a lot of money.

If you have a grill or smoker of any sort, invest in a cover to keep it from getting dirty or damaged when it isn't in use. I'd definitely put this closer to the kitchen to save you valuable time walking back and forth from the kitchen to the grill. Keep all accessories stored nearby, and be sure to clean it well after each use. I'm not personally a fan of electric grills, but charcoal and gas each have their pros and cons. I've also seen grills hooked up to natural gas lines, which makes grilling a lot easier than changing out a propane tank every time you want to cook.

Keep in mind that it can get very windy outside, so when you know there's a storm about to hit, be sure to secure any umbrellas, shade sails, and anything light, so they won't blow away, and keep awnings closed when they're not in use.

You can always use candles for nighttime lighting, but be sure to blow them out when you're done. If you can get a small fire pit, these are great when hanging out with friends or on a weekend night for toasting marshmallows with a glass of wine. The outdoor string lights are charming and a nice addition.

## Gardening

If having a garden interests you, think about what you want to grow: flowers, vegetables, and/or herbs. If you're aiming to cultivate edible plants, the closer to the kitchen your herb garden is, the better, so you're not making unnecessarily long trips.

A lot of useful herbs like basil, thyme, and rosemary really thrive outdoors. Consider a potted herb garden, but only plant what you will use, what is easy to care for, and what will thrive in your climate and yard with the amount of sunlight your area gets.

It's helpful for monitoring your soil content and easy on the eyes, as well as your back, if you can box your garden area off and raise the beds, especially if you have uneven terrain. This can make for a pleasing aesthetic and make it easier to control what you have growing. The closer the plants are to your hose, or whatever you plan to use for irrigation, the better. Keep all of your gardening tools and supplies close together in a shed if you have one, or at the very least have a few shelves near the house so they're not just propped up against the walls.

Although a nice, green lawn and a blooming garden can be beautiful, they become a lot harder to maintain the larger they get and if you have pets. Large dogs especially tend to wear down lawns when they're playing outside, and dogs do like to dig in the dirt. If you would rather have furry friends than a lawn, you know yourself best, but know that even if you keep your dog indoors most of the day, they will need to play outside eventually, so there's a good chance your lawn won't hold up. If you decide to go this route, be sure and pick up any litter the dog leaves behind and keep your yard free of hazards.

## Pools

Depending on how you take care of it, pools can either make a home significantly more inviting or significantly less inviting. If you've recently moved into a place with a pool that is proving to be too much for you to take care of, it may be worth looking into having it removed and replaced with something you would actually use. If you do choose to keep your pool functional, be sure and check the water quality daily, check backwash filters as instructed in the manuals, and skim it for bugs, which can add up quickly. If you're in a condo that has a pool, take advantage of this feature and go hang out during the off hours. An early-morning swim or hanging out after dinner for a late-day swim is good exercise and a good way to spend time outdoors. Never swim alone and be sure children are constantly supervised around any water.

### Bonus Tips & Tricks

❑ Gardening, walks, swimming, outdoor meals, and sitting under the stars can all help us to feel more grounded, grateful, and peaceful.

❑ Trees are nice, but make sure they don't make a mess of your furniture before installing anything permanent directly under them.

❑ If you have autumn and deciduous trees where you live, rake the area thoroughly when the trees shed their leaves.

# AFTERWORD

It looks like you've completed all of the chapters in this book! Well done! Remember that a clean and well-organized home should be what you're aiming for, not a perfect home. No home is perfect, nor should it be. But it should be easy to maintain, clean, and organize, and it should also be a space that you *like* to be in. You can make that happen, and you can keep it clean and organized by putting things away when you're done with them and by planning your weeks and working your plan.

Spend a few minutes every day cleaning up after yourself; planning for tomorrow and the upcoming week will serve you well moving forward. For instance, taking fifteen minutes each day to run the vacuum, dust something that needs to be dusted, clean off your stove, wipe a refrigerator shelf, clear out a drawer, or clean off a shelf will reward you tenfold. You get the drill! No one is going to do this for you, so get to it before it gets out of hand and overwhelming!

Since you're the one who knows your taste and abilities best and what is now in your space, it's impossible for a book like this one to tell you exactly what color scheme you should use in each room or how you should be placing your furniture for maximum comfort, ease of use, and utility. Luckily, you can call in resources and professionals like me if you're truly stumped and need a little extra help.

As a final note, remember that homes, like people, are organic and constantly changing with us and our needs. Things will always need to be replaced and repaired and cleaned. That's part of the responsibility and joy of having things. You take the time to take care of something, and it will be there for you, right where you intentionally decided to store it. People will come in and out of our living spaces as well, so embrace your home and whom you share it with to its fullest! It's important to revisit what you learned here every so often as your tastes change and you move to new places over the years. Keep in mind, if any room gets out of control, the first step is to realize that you most likely have too many things and to take responsibility for your space. With regular cleaning and putting things away after you use them, your efforts will be rewarded each time you come home. Thank you so much for taking the time to read this book, and I wish you and your loved ones peaceful, beautiful living.

# ABOUT THE AUTHOR

*A* bachelor's degree in engineering, and certifications in staging, interior redesign, one day decorating, and paint color all support my love of creating beautiful, welcoming, and functional spaces. My top priorities when evaluating a space are addressing any problematic areas head-on with innovative solutions, making sure my design plan accentuates the positive features of the room, and that the pieces are scaled properly for the space.

My cousin Carol Tierney and I have partnered to provide organizational services to help clients clear their spaces and reclaim their homes, one room at a time. We both know that small changes create a sizable impact.

I appreciate every client and the trust they have in me to help them, whether they are selling a property or restyling and organizing their space. Please feel free to visit my website at www.StagingAndStylingSpaces.com.